A

People Against the Press

People Against the Press

An Enquiry into the Press Council

Geoffrey Robertson

Quartet Books
London Melbourne New York

First published by Quartet Books Limited 1983
A member of the Namara Group
27/29 Goodge Street, London W1P 1FD

Copyright © 1983 by Geoffrey Robertson

British Library Cataloguing in Publication Data

Robertson, Geoffrey
  People against the press.
  1. Press Council
  I. Title
070'.06'041   PN5118

ISBN 0-7043-2384-2

Typeset by MC Typeset, Chatham, Kent
Printed and bound in Great Britain
by Mackays of Chatham Limited, Kent

Contents

Acknowledgements

This book arises from the work of a number of individuals who met as a group in 1981–2 to study the performance of the Press Council. The group was chaired by the author, and comprised Sarah Boston, Geoffrey Drain, Jacob Ecclestone, Geoffrey Goodman, Richard Hoggart, John Monks, Russell Profitt, Muriel Turner, Phillip Whitehead and Katherine Whitehorn. The enquiry was initiated by the action of the Campaign for Press Freedom, which brought the group together on the understanding that it would be entirely independent of that or any other organization. It proceeded without any assistance outside the resources of its own members. A number of people who had complained to the Press Council in recent years were contacted and invited to submit evidence, and gratitude is expressed to the seventy-seven of them, listed in Appendix B, who responded in detail to this request. Graeme Adkin, Heather Rogers and Jo-anne Winston assisted the author's researches; Julian Disney, Jane Cousins, Andrew Nicol and Jeremy Tunstall offered valuable criticism of the draft, and Claire Davis worked on the manuscript with Janet Law and Chris Parker of Quartet Books. Jeananne Crowley is particularly deserving of acknowledgement.

Introduction

The Press Council was established in 1953. Since then, it has changed its character more dramatically than the newspapers whose ethics it affects to supervise. It began as a proprietorial concession to parliamentary pressure: a handful of experienced newspapermen who occasionally deigned to criticize, ever so tactfully, displays of bad manners in popular papers. Today, it is a much more portentous organization: eighteen representatives of the people, and eighteen representatives of the press, joined together under the chairmanship of a distinguished lawyer to pass judgement upon hundreds of complaints each year, to pronounce regularly upon newspaper ethics, to defend freedom of expression and to warn against the encroachment of media monopolies. These, at least, are its self-appointed tasks, and scarcely a week passes without reports of its latest activity featuring in some of the newspapers whose owners finance its operations. In column inches, the Press Council is one of Britain's most newsworthy private organizations. Whether it has succeeded in making the news worthy, by combating bias and distortion and inaccuracy in the British press, is the question to which this study is directed.

The Press Council deserves recognition as an institution designed to serve an important political purpose, namely to protect the newspaper industry from legislation which would curb its freedom and its powers. It functions as a device for condemning journalistic misbehaviour of a kind which, if left undeterred, would almost certainly be curbed by Act of Parliament. That is the reason why the council was established, and why it has been expanded and democratized. Press proprietors do not pay several hundred thousand pounds each year just for the pleasure of having their newspapers publicly castigated: they invest in an organization whose existence offers a form of insurance against the advent of laws which would otherwise be designed, for example, to safeguard personal privacy, to prohibit cheque-book journalism, or to guarantee a right of reply. The purpose of the Press Council is to prove to the public that reliance upon a system of voluntary self-regulation is better than recourse to a set of statutory principles, powers and penalties.

The argument for keeping media law at bay is exceptionally strong. The tentacles of official secrecy, contempt, copyright and confidence already smother far too much public-interest reporting. Politicians made an appalling mess of their last major attempt at media regulation – the 1981 Contempt of Court Act – and many believe that their efforts at drafting a 'right of reply' statute or a privacy law would prove just as ham-fisted. Even more worrying is the prospect that parliament might establish a statutory body with broad powers to control the press and to expel 'unprofessional' journalists. If political interference with television programmes by the Independent Broadcasting Authority provides insufficient evidence of the potential danger, the Steyn Commission in South Africa has produced a blueprint for government control of the press, through a council with statutory powers to fine and suspend and expel journalists deemed guilty of 'improper conduct'. If the existence of the Press Council justifies the argument against such expedients, then for this relief it deserves much thanks.

But for the argument against legal control to be valid, the Press Council must genuinely offer a speedy and effective remedy for distortion and inaccuracy. It must lay down authoritative principles on invasion of privacy and cheque-book journalism and the right of reply, and its principles must be respected and applied. Its boast that it maintains and improves the ethical standards of the British press must be capable of proof. All this, and more, it must achieve without legal powers, public funding, or even contractual arrangements with its constituent newspapers. These are formidable obstacles, and it would not be a matter for surprise if the council failed to overcome them. The consequences of failure, however, are so serious that all who wish the press well should be concerned to detect inadequacies in the council's performance, and to examine alternative or supplementary methods of achieving its undoubtedly valuable objectives.

These consequences have been emphasized by recent

demands from different parts of the political spectrum for some form of disciplinary sanction over newspapers, or at least over the editors and journalists who work for them. The Labour Party, in its official policy document (1983), proclaimed its intention to replace the Press Council with a 'stronger, more representative body', and to introduce a statutory right of reply.[1] For the Alliance, Mrs Shirley Williams MP has demanded that the Press Council 'must be stronger, must have further sanctions, and must be more forceful about the way it goes about its business'.[2] Sir David Napley doubtless speaks for many fellow lawyers when he advocates 'a disciplinary body empowered to suspend journalists from the practice of their craft'.[3] A recent book by Major-General Richard Clutterbuck argues for an 'Institute for the Mass Media', with power to strike journalists off its register for disobedience to a binding professional code, and even for the offence of 'conniving at disobedience to police instructions' in certain circumstances.[4] The Press Council, which has no power beyond the force of its own arguments, devotes much of its publicity to resisting those who would thrust legal powers upon it.

Journalism is not a profession. It is the exercise by occupation of the right to free expression available to every citizen. That right, being available to all, cannot in principle be withdrawn from a few by any system of licensing or professional registration. This was last attempted by Cromwell, in 1643, who appointed twenty-seven licensors chosen from 'the good and the wise' – schoolmasters, lawyers, ministers of religion and doctors – who ordered books and newspapers containing political errors to be burned by the public hangman. The system became a means of fraud and political favouritism, and was abolished in 1695, having achieved little more than the inspiration of an immortal argument against its very existence, Milton's 'Areopagitica': 'The attempt to keep out evil doctrine by licensing is like the exploit of that gallant man who thought to keep out the crows by shutting his park gate . . .'. The Press Council attempts to keep them out by dressing up as a scarecrow. But whom, exactly, does it frighten?

Newspaper proprietors, who pay for it, have been given little cause for anxiety. It has not opposed with great vigour or any success the tendencies towards concentration of newspaper holdings. Journalists, who have most to gain by supporting an institution active in the defence of press freedom, have withdrawn from it en masse. In 1980, the National Union of Journalists declared it to be 'wholly ineffective' and 'incapable of reform'. Editors, who are meant to fear it, often react with indifference, hostility or contempt to adverse adjudications. Most (but not all) editors will publish Press Council judgements, although often without prominence and in shortened form. Rarely is publication attended by apology, editorial soul-searching, or follow-up features: the content of the ethical standards being developed by the Press Council does not seem of very much public interest in the eyes of the press. Unless, of course, an editor chooses to trumpet his own defiance. In October 1982, for example, the Press Council issued a detailed and resounding condemnation of the *Sun* for publishing a sensationalized, distorted and racially emotive account of a demonstration by black people. That newspaper responded with a front-page repetition of the article's original allegations, a savage editorial attack on those who had dared to report it to the council and a perverse boast that 'the *Sun* is flattered to be singled out as the target for complaint'.[5] There are numerous examples of successful complaints backfiring in this fashion. When the editor of the *Sunday Express*, Sir John Junor, was admonished for publishing a racial slur in his own column, he repeated the offensive comment in the next edition, with a side-swipe at the 'po-faced, pompous, pin-striped, humourless twits who sit on the Press Council'.[6]

This lack of respect for the Press Council in the industry which it serves has had predictable consequences. When newspapers flouted its declaration of principle on cheque-book journalism after the arrest of Peter Sutcliffe, the 'Yorkshire Ripper', their behaviour was an important factor in persuading parliament to approve the more draconian sections of the Contempt of Court Act, which have measurably reduced the freedom of the media to report matters of public interest. But when the Press Council finally censured their conduct, in February 1983, the worst offenders were unrepentant. The report was described as 'short-term, short-sighted and smug', by Sir David English, the editor of the *Daily Mail,* who had been strongly criticized. For English, the criticism 'proves yet again that the Press Council still does not truly understand the concept of a Free Press'.[7] The Press Council is funded by newspaper publishers: its purpose is to avoid the need for further legislative controls. Ironically, its present failure to command respect has become a persuasive argument *for* statutory control.

These developments would be doubly disturbing if the Press Council was deserving of the respect and obedience to which it lays claim. In view of the unique nature of its work, it is odd that there has been so little independent assessment of its operations. Part of the reason for the absence both of critical comment and public appreciation may be the council's extraordinary habit of presenting its annual reports three to four years after the period with which they deal. This study was commenced in 1981, on the basis of its 1977 report. In July 1982 the council published its report for the year 1978. Its report on press conduct and developments in 1979 emerged in November 1982. These reports were largely digests of adjudications delivered during the year in question. The only book on the subject, Phillip Levy's *The Press Council*, was published in 1967 and is now out of date and out of print.[8] The Australian Journalists' Association has sent a working party to study the council's impact on the press in Britain: it concluded that the council had not measurably reduced sensationalism and distortion, or political bias or tendencies towards press monopoly. Its adjudications were couched in the 'muffled tones of an apologist'.

There has only been one recent study of any significance: a chapter on the council in the Report of the third Royal Commission on the Press, which was published in 1977. The commission concluded: 'It is unhappily certain that the Council has so far failed to persuade the knowledgeable public that it deals satisfactorily with complaints against newspapers, notwithstanding that this has come to be seen as its main purpose.'[9] It made no less than eighteen recommendations for improving the council's performance. A few of these have been adopted but their effect has not been analysed.

This book is an attempt to measure the achievements of the Press Council against its own constitutional objectives, and to draw from the shortfall a set of recommendations which would more satisfactorily reconcile the right to freedom of expression with the right of persons whose conduct or reputation is misrepresented in the exercise of that freedom to have the record set straight.

The enquiry began as an examination of the council's response to the strictures passed upon it by the third Royal Commission on the Press. However, it was soon found unrealistic to examine the Press Council's performance in isolation, without considering the law of defamation, which offers in some cases an alternative system of redress for victims of media distortion. Another necessary perspective was supplied by a study of comparable organizations in Britain (notably the Advertising Standards

Authority and the Broadcasting Complaints Commission) and by comparing similar systems which operate in European countries.

The most illuminating evidence received in the course of the enquiry came from individuals and organizations who had complained to the Press Council about newspaper errors and ethics. In 1981 a large number of people who had used the council's services were contacted and asked to comment on their experiences. This consumer survey revealed how the council's complaints machinery works in practice. The most compelling criticisms of its procedures were made by successful complainants, rather than by those whose submissions had been rejected. Thus the survey, set out in detail in Chapter 3, is not a record of axe-grinding: it is a remarkable account of a complaints commission the majority of whose beneficiaries said they were dissatisfied with the benefits they received.

Although the book is necessarily critical of many facets of the Press Council's performance, it is undeniable that the council's members and officers genuinely try to maintain and improve the ethical performance of the British press. Its thirty-six individual members give up their time without payment, and do their best to see that justice is done between complainant and newspaper. Many of the council's shortcomings are explained by its lack of resources and its voluntary composition. Its chairman is part-time, and it has only eleven paid employees, most of them engaged on clerical duties. It normally meets, as a council, only once every two months. Yet it assumes the mantle of a court deciding cases against the British press, a legislature decreeing rules for editors and journalists, a guardian of traditional freedom of expression, and a watchdog barking against concentrations of press ownership. It is not surprising if it fails in these self-appointed tasks: what is surprising is that it should attempt them with such minimal resources.

But if the Press Council creates public expectations which it cannot fulfil, the representatives of the public will seek other methods of fulfilling them – methods which may impose statutory responsibility at the expense of public-interest reporting. Yet these public expectations are not unreasonable. The third Royal Commission, which had great sympathy for the press, nevertheless discovered 'flagrant breaches of acceptable standards' and 'inexcusable intrusions into privacy'.[10] The record since then shows that the Press Council has not adjudicated public complaints speedily or effectively, its principles on cheque-book journalism, privacy and the right of reply have been continually flouted, and it has been incapable of defending press freedom against serious encroachments or of making any impact in warning against press monopolies. The question, at the end of the day, is not whether the Press Council does good, but whether the good that it manages to do within its present limitations is good enough to justify its claim to hold a fair balance between the press and the people.

1
Press Council History

The idea that disputes over the contents of newspapers might be resolved by some independent but non-legal body developed first in Sweden, where publishers and journalists established a 'Press Fair Practice' Board in 1916. This initiative went unnoticed in Britain, where newspaper comment was constrained by severe laws of libel and contempt. But the performance of the national press after the lifting of wartime censorship in 1945 brought the issue of press freedom and responsibility before parliament at the insistence of the National Union of Journalists (NUJ), dismayed at the growth of monopolies and at proprietorial pressures upon editors and journalists.

The First Royal Commission

The parliamentary debates which led to the establishment of the first Royal Commission on the Press in 1947 articulated the criticisms which are still made today: the decline in the number of national newspapers, the concentration of ownership in the provincial press, the suppression and distortion of news for politically partisan or commercial reasons, and the decline in the calibre of personnel. One journalist MP, Michael Foot, claimed that some editors were merely 'stooges, cyphers and sycophants'. As a consequence of these debates, a Royal Commission was appointed 'with the object of furthering the free expression of opinion through the Press and the greatest practicable accuracy in the presentation of news'.[1]

The Royal Commission, reporting in 1949, found some evidence to support the allegations of political bias, misrepresentation and inaccuracy. It pointed with surprise to the failure of the press to safeguard its standards of performance, or to foster any sense of responsibility to the public. At the suggestion of the NUJ, it recommended the establishment of 'A General Council of the Press', which would work to obtain agreement upon what constitutes sound professional practice, and would seek to eradicate discreditable behaviour. In particular, it should operate to discourage intrusions upon privacy, to correct misstatements of fact, and to encourage the provision of space in newspapers for the expression of views contrary to those promoted by the paper. Such a General Council, 'by censuring undesirable types of journalistic conduct and by all other possible means, should build up a code of conduct in accordance with the highest professional standards'.[2]

Significantly, the Royal Commission rejected calls for a closed professional association which might license journalists or expel them from practice. It was divided, however, upon the question of whether the council should be given statutory powers like the General Medical Council, or rely solely upon moral authority. The majority of the commission preferred a voluntary body, 'which would derive its authority from the press itself, and not from statute'. It added that the public confidence and support which it would need in order to be fully effective would require that a chairman and a proportion of the council be drawn from outside the press.

The Royal Commission envisaged a body of far greater authority than the Press Council is now, or ever has been. Its 'General Council of the Press' was to be the *governing* body of the profession, regulating recruitment and training, negotiating pension schemes, and representing the press in negotiations with the government and with international agencies. As such, its edicts on professional conduct were to have the force of rulings by the General Medical Council or the Law Society, albeit not backed by statutory powers of discipline. It was to have sufficient resources to promote consumer studies, to provide early warnings of monopolistic tendencies, to oversee the training of journalists, and to research the long-term social and economic development of the industry.

But after the commission reported in 1949, no governing body emerged. Four years were spent in desultory and unenthusiastic discussions between proprietors, until in 1952 a private member's bill was introduced in parliament to set up a statutory council.[3] This prospect brought a speedy end to discussions, and the establishment by the industry of a General Council of the

Press, which commenced operations in 1953. Its main objectives were:

- to preserve the established freedom of the British press;
- to maintain the character of the British press in accordance with the highest professional and commercial standards;
- to keep under review any developments likely to restrict the supply of information of public interest and importance.

The first General Council was the palest reflection of the Royal Commission's recommendations. It had no lay membership, and its first chairman was the then proprietor of *The Times*. The annual reports for its first decade of operation were slim volumes which had little impact. Doubtless it did its best, with a small staff and a small budget (£4100 – contributed principally by associations representing proprietors of national and provincial newspapers) to resolve ethical problems and to warn against legal encroachments on free speech. Many of its early rulings appear today to be overly sensitive to government and the aristocracy, otherwise contrary to the public interest, or faintly ridiculous. Its first declaration was that a *Daily Mirror* readership poll on the question of whether Princess Margaret should be allowed, if she so desired, to marry Group-Captain Townsend, was 'contrary to the best traditions of British journalism'.[4] Its discoveries of press inaccuracy and misrepresentation were greeted by the offending newspapers with at most expressions of polite regret. Its lack of relevance to Fleet Street after five years of operation was exemplified in the reply of doughty *Sunday Express* columnist John Gordon to a reader who had threatened to report him to the council for failure to publish a justified factual correction: 'You can report me to the Press Council, Madame Tussaud's, the Society for the Protection of Sputniks, NATO, UNESCO or the Dancing Dervishes' Association as you wish. May you enjoy yourself.'

The Second Royal Commission

The poor performance of the Press Council was subjected to scathing criticism by the second Royal Commission on the Press, chaired by Lord Shawcross, which reported in 1962. Shawcross deplored the council's failure to implement the first Royal Commission's recommendations. He castigated its refusal to appoint lay members, and derided the 'bald factual accounts', devoid of any perspective or analysis, which served as the council's annual contribution to the study of press economics and ownership. The second Royal Commission delivered a stern ultimatum: either the Press Council reform itself as a matter of urgency, or the government should step in to establish a statutory body:

> We do not disagree with the conclusion of the 1949 Commission that there are important advantages in a body of this kind resting upon a voluntary basis and deriving its authority not from statute but from the Press itself. If however the Press is not willing to invest the Council with the necessary authority and to contribute the necessary finance the case for a statutory body with definite powers and the right to levy the industry is a clear one. In our view all the interests concerned should consider as a matter of urgency the revision of the Council's constitution so as both to comply with the recommendations of the 1949 Commission as to membership and objects and to ensure that the Council would have the necessary powers, including the power to call for information about ownership and control, and funds to enable it to carry out all its objectives to the fullest degree. We do not think that the absence of an enabling statute need necessarily be fatal to the activities of such a body. Much of its power could rest upon a contractual basis. We think that the Press should be given another opportunity itself voluntarily to establish an authoritative General Council with a lay element as recommended by the 1949 Commission. We recommend, however, that the Government should specify a time limit after which legislation would be introduced for the establishment of such a body, if in the meantime it had not been set up voluntarily.[5]

The important suggestion that the Press Council could derive power from binding contracts will be considered in more detail in Chapter 7. The newspaper societies which funded the council did not take up this suggestion, but they did rapidly implement some radical changes. It is clear that, once again, it was the threat of legislation which secured reform. The title 'General Council of the Press' was abandoned in favour of the less assuming 'Press Council', and the chairman and 20% of the members were appointed from outside the newspaper industry. In 1964 Lord Devlin, a retired law lord of great distinction and considerable literary prowess, was appointed chairman and under his leadership the council adopted an altogether more impressive tone and authority. It began to reprimand press misconduct in positive terms, and issued weighty Declarations of Principle. At the same time it delivered magisterial defences of press conduct against government bluff and bluster – notably the Wilson government's attempt to stop journalists from interviewing witnesses to the Aberfan disaster in 1966, and its attempt to use the 'D Notice' system in 1967 to cover up MI6 interception of private telegrams. A feature of this vigorous period under the leadership of Lord Devlin and then another distinguished judge, Lord Pearce, was the council's concern for press freedom, evidenced in its booklets, 'Contempt of Court' (1967), 'Privacy' (1971) and 'Defamation' (1973).

It was perhaps inevitable, given the higher profile it took on issues of press freedom, that it should be publicly perceived more as a champion of the press than as a watchdog for the public. This was certainly the view of the Younger Committee on Privacy, which analysed the council's performance on that subject in 1973. It noted that the council's first concern was to preserve press freedom. The committee added: 'We do not see how the Council can expect to command public confidence in its ability to take account of the reactions of the public unless it has at least an equal membership of persons who are qualified to speak for the public at large.'[6] It made two further recommendations: that the council should insist that its adjudications be published with a prominence equal to that given to the original offending article, and that it should codify its adjudications on privacy and keep the code up to date. Neither of these recommendations has been implemented.

The Third Royal Commission

The first detailed study of the operations of the Press Council was conducted by the third Royal Commission on the Press, chaired by Lord McGregor, which was established in 1974 and which reported in 1977. While paying a measure of tribute to the work of the council, the commission's criticisms were both authoritative and far-reaching. 'It is unhappily certain,' it stated, 'that the Council has so far failed to persuade the knowledgeable public that it deals satisfactorily with complaints against newspapers.' It identified a number of factors which had contributed to this lack of confidence.

Partisanship The council's role as an advocate for press freedom detracted from its claim to be an impartial adjudicating body. Its director had displayed 'an impatience with public comment on the performance of the press', and some of its statements were couched in 'the language of partisanship which inevitably weakens confidence in the impartiality of the Press Council'.[7]

The legal waiver The Press Council's insistence that a complainant sign away his or her legal rights against the newspaper, before the Press Council would proceed to an adjudication, gave an impression that: 'The Press Council is more concerned to protect the newspapers from the public than to raise the standards of the newspapers in the interests of the public.'[8]

The lack of clear standards The Royal Commission concluded, from an examination of Press Council adjudications, that 'the standards they apply and the terms in which they are expressed fall short of what is desirable. In particular, we consider that adjudications do not contain sufficient argument, and that they sometimes make too many allowances for editorial discretion and errors of fact.' The commission recommended in the strongest terms that the Press Council should draw up a code of conduct, both to inform editors and journalists of the standards they should strive to attain, and to enable the public at large to judge the performance of the press by known and accepted ethical values.[9]

Refusal to condemn inaccuracy and distortion The commission pointed out that the Press Council does not regard 'inaccuracy' as good ground for complaint, unless it is proved to arise from malice or recklessness. At the same time, the council consistently defended the right of newspapers to be politically partisan. 'In other words,' the commission said, 'the Council leaves newspapers free to present contentious opinions on the basis of inaccurate reports.' In consequence, the commission thought that the council was not strict enough 'to protect the public against the dangers of partisan opinion exacerbated by factual inaccuracy'.[10]

Ineffectiveness of council sanctions The commission found evidence of 'flagrant breaches of acceptable standards' and 'inexcusable intrusions into privacy'. 'We feel strongly,' it stated, 'that the Press Council should have more power over the Press

. . . . There is a pressing call to enhance the standing of the Press Council in the eyes of the public and potential complainants.'[11]

Like its two predecessors, the third Royal Commission found the press wanting. And, like them, it reached for the same broad solution: the press must put its own house in order, because 'willingness on the part of the Press to accept and conform to the rulings of the Council is the only alternative to the introduction of a legal right of privacy, and, perhaps, of a statutory Press Council'. Thus the same stick which had been waved in threatening fashion by Royal Commissions in 1949 and 1962 was brought out of the cupboard in 1977. 'Behave – or else.' Like its predecessors, the third Commission did little to define the 'or else'. Instead, it recommended a package of reforms in the council. In order 'to fulfil the hopes that were held for it in 1949', the Press Council should:

- be supplied with more staff and money to advertise its services;
- obtain undertakings from newspapers that they would publish upheld complaints on their front page;
- initiate more complaints itself, especially by way of monitoring and publicizing the record of persistent offenders;
- support an effective right of reply;
- produce a written code of conduct for journalists;
- express its condemnation of journalistic misbehaviour in a more forthright way;
- supply more detailed reasons for its decisions;
- take a stronger line on inaccuracy and bias;
- reconsider, with a view to abandoning, the legal waiver.

The report of the third Royal Commission on the Press was published in July 1977. It had little impact, either generally or in relation to its criticisms of the Press Council. Some adjustments to the composition of the council were made, so that half of its membership is now drawn from the lay public, and a former journalist was appointed as a 'conciliator' to try to negotiate settlements before complaints were formally adjudicated. The council's considered response to the commission's proposals was not published until four years later when, in July 1981, it released its annual report for the eighteen months which had ended in December 1978. It specifically rejected the idea of a code, the need to seek more funds and publicity for its services, and the suggestion that it should seek undertakings from newspapers to give front-page prominence to complaints upheld against them. The legal waiver remains, as does the council's refusal to monitor newspapers.

Recent Developments

In 1980 the NUJ, the organization which first prompted the Press Council's formation and which had always contributed funds and members, withdrew entirely from its operations, announcing that the council was 'incapable of reform'. This loss of support from most working journalists was a serious blow to the credibility of the council, a blow not anticipated by the third Royal Commission. The decision to withdraw was taken at the union's Annual Delegate Meeting after two years of debate over the value of continuing membership. The inadequacies of the Press Council were denounced at Trades Union Congress conferences in 1980 and 1981, most vociferously by representatives of the print unions, thereby signalling further loss of support from within the newspaper industry. The 1982 TUC conference, however, saw the dramatic appearance of a 'non-aggression pact' between the Press Council and the TUC. The TUC agreed to put pressure on the NUJ to rejoin the Press Council, in return for three Press Council 'concessions': it would try to speed up its procedures; it would attempt to codify its past decisions, and it would ask newspapers to publish its adjudications with 'reasonable prominence'.[12] Critics pointed out that the very next Press Council adjudication involved a fifteen-month delay; that the council had always rejected demands for 'front-page prominence', and that the compilation of the 'code' (which might turn out to be no more than a résumé of decisions) was to be undertaken by a former director who had once declared: 'I believe it would be a disastrous mistake to move in the direction of setting up any kind of code of conduct for the press.'[13] Others were surprised that three such elementary reforms should come, (if they were to come at all), not from the Press Council's initiative to improve its own performance, but only by way of a bargaining and negotiating process with the TUC.

In 1983 the council faced three severe tests of its credibility as an alternative to legal regulation. The first came with the publication of its report on 'Press Conduct in the Sutcliffe Case', which castigated national newspapers for offering blood money to relatives and friends of the mass murderer. It swiftly became apparent that this two-year enquiry was incomplete. Although the report was valuable in exposing some conduct of questionable morality, its conclusions were unacceptable to the press in principle and unenforceable in practice. The second reading of a Bill to give a legal right to reply to victims of press distortion provided an occasion for serious criticism of the council by MPs from all parties. The Bill was narrowly rejected, after the government indicated that it would not support such legislation 'until we are quite satisfied that the Press Council is not able to deal with these matters properly'.[14] It was not clear how the level of government satisfaction was to be measured; for the purposes of this debate the Secretary of State simply accepted the Press Council's familiar promises, regularly made since 1975 but never delivered, that it would take steps to improve its efficiency. In April 1983 the NUJ conference resoundingly rejected a TUC-inspired call to rejoin the Press Council. Representatives of the journalists whose ethics the council affects to regulate found nothing in its recent performance to change their view that it should not be taken seriously.

Conclusion

The Press Council is, historically, a product of the newspaper industry's fear of statutory regulation. Three Royal Commissions have found unacceptable professional behaviour in Fleet Street and the provincial press. The first suggested a voluntarily-supported 'General Council of the Press' as the alternative to legislation. When, and only when, legislation was threatened, the council made its appearance as a small private body funded by newspaper proprietors. Its work was judged by the second Royal Commission to be cosmetic and ineffectual. That commission gave it an ultimatum: increase your power and public confidence, or be swept away by legislation. The newspaper industry became alarmed; it responded by providing lay members, a distinguished judicial chairman, and a large infusion of funds. The consequence was initially impressive: the Press Council became an eloquent spokesman for press interests, and its adjudications, under the guidance of Lords Devlin and Pearce, were respected, if not always obeyed, by the press. Its high profile on issues of press freedom, however, caused it to be seen as less than impartial in dealing with public complaints. In 1974 Lord Shawcross became chairman, resigning directorships of Times Newspapers and Thames Television in order to do so.

He was an advocate, not a judge, and his annual reports were outspokenly partisan and moralistic. He put the council's case to the third Royal Commission, a case which was defensive and opposed to reform. That Royal Commission demanded substantial reforms, and reminded the council once again that the inevitable alternative to a strong Press Council was legislation. A few of the reforms were immediately implemented, some were promised in an ambiguous way to the TUC five years later, but most have not been implemented.

There was no sign of the TUC-inspired reforms at the time this book went to press, six months after they had been promised. The promises made to the government before the 'right to reply' debate about reforms in speed and efficiency were unspecific and equally unforthcoming. Any plans for change in the Press Council in 1983, its thirtieth anniversary, were not apparent from its most recent Annual Report, that for the year 1979, which was published at the end of 1982. The chairman devoted his foreword to rejecting the idea that the council might acquire any sort of power to implement or enforce its rulings. There was 'no prospect whatever' of the industry volunteering to accept Press Council sanctions, and any scheme imposed on the press by legislation would necessarily imperil press freedom. 'May the Press Council be spared teeth for many years to come' was the chairman's hope for the council's future. [15]

2
The Council at Work

The Press Council occupies a small mock-Georgian building in Salisbury Square, just off Fleet Street. It is a private and voluntary association, subscribed to by seven organizations: five of them represent the owners of newspapers and journals in the UK, and the others are the Guild of British Newspaper Editors and the Institute of Journalists. The council has eleven full-time staff, a paid but part-time chairman, and thirty-six members. Eighteen of them are selected by an Appointments Commission as representatives of the public, while the other half are directors or employees of press organizations, nominated to the council by its constituent bodies. The full council meets once every two months, but most members also serve on one of its three committees which meet each month to consider public complaints. Although the processing and adjudication of these complaints forms 80% of the council's business, its constitutional objectives are much more far-reaching. They are:

(i) To preserve the established freedom of the British Press.
(ii) To maintain the character of the British Press in accordance with the highest professional and commercial standards.
(iii) To consider complaints about the conduct of the Press or the conduct of persons and organisations towards the Press; to deal with these complaints in whatever manner might seem practical and appropriate and record resultant action.
(iv) To keep under review developments likely to restrict the supply of information of public interest and importance.
(v) To report publicly on developments that may tend towards greater concentration or monopoly in the Press (including changes in ownership, control and growth of press

undertakings) and to publish statistical information relating thereto.

(vi) To make representations on appropriate occasions to the Government, organs of the United Nations and the Press organisations abroad.

(vii) To publish periodical reports recording the Council's work and to review from time to time, developments in the Press and the factors affecting them.

The performance of the council in fulfilling each of these tasks is assessed in the chapters which follow. The present chapter examines the council's basic structure and the formal procedures which it has developed to deal with the objectives of its constitution.

Funding

The council's constituent bodies, and the financial contributions they made in the twelve months up to the end of December 1979 (the date of the latest published figures) are as follows:[1]

The Newspaper Publishers' Association	£79,998

(An organization which represents the owners of national newspapers)

The Newspaper Society	£50,803

(An organization which represents the owners of provincial newspapers. There is some overlap with the NPA – e.g. Associated Newspapers, which owns the Daily Mail *and a string of provincial papers, belongs to both groups)*

Periodical Publishers' Association Ltd	£8980

(It represents, as its name suggests, the publishers of periodical journals)

The Scottish Daily Newspaper Society	£4078

(An organization representing the interests of publishers of daily newspapers in Scotland)

Scottish Newspaper Proprietors' Association	£2629

(Representing the owners of weekly and bi-weekly Scottish papers)

The Institute of Journalists	£1882

(A trade union with approximately 2500 journalist members)

The Guild of British Newspaper Editors	£1255
(A body of editors, mainly of provincial newspapers)	
The National Union of Journalists	£6119
(A trade union representing about 32,000 working journalists. It withdrew from membership in 1980)	
Total	£155,744

It can be seen that the Press Council is now funded almost entirely by press proprietors. Its budget is largely taken up by salaries and administrative expenses, leaving little space for advertising or investigation of complaints. Its income and its staff are only one-third the size of the budget and personnel commanded by the Advertising Standards Authority (ASA), a similar voluntary body established and financed by the advertising industry to maintain ethical standards in newspaper advertisements. The third Royal Commission recommended that the Press Council should seek more funds to enable it to increase staff and to advertise its services, in the same way as does the ASA. In response to this recommendation, the Press Council conceded that 'it is well known the Council could be better known', but rejected the proposal, on the grounds that it 'would require the constituent bodies to provide very much more money than they currently do and the Council is firmly opposed to any suggestion that an approach be made to the Government for public money'.[2] One way in which proprietors could meet part of the commission's recommendation would be for them to donate space for advertisements of the council's services. Indeed, many have sponsored free advertisements for the ASA, to such an extent that their generosity quadrupled the money value of the authority's advertising campaign in 1981. There is no reason why they should not equally be prepared to donate space to enable the Press Council to become effective by advertising its services. The fact that readers of a council advertisement would be told how to lodge a complaint against the newspaper which carried it should not be a deterrent, if the sponsors of the Press Council really believe in its work.

Membership

The seven funding organizations nominate a total of eighteen members of the council. A further eighteen members, who serve for a renewable term of three years, are drawn from the public.

They are selected by an Appointments Commission, comprising five persons who are not otherwise connected with the Press Council. The members of the Appointments Commission are, however, selected by the Press Council, and the council's director acts as secretary to the commission. There are no particular qualifications for lay membership, although the third Royal Commission recommended that the Appointments Commission should 'seek to achieve as wide a range of members as possible, in age, career, background and part of the country'.[4] Of the thirty-one public representatives appointed between 1970 and 1980, twenty-seven were aged over forty, twenty-two lived 'below the Wash', and only one – a gas engineer – could be described as a 'blue-collar' worker. The favoured occupations were clergyman (three), company executive (three), civic dignitary (four), headmistress (two), lecturer (four), trade-union official (three), civil servant (two), and the professions (four).

In 1980 the council made a conscious and commendable effort to broaden the social range of its lay membership. It widely advertised its vacant positions, and applications jumped from forty-four in 1978 to 580 in 1981 and 655 in 1982. By the end of 1982 it had six women, five trade unionists and one Asian amongst its members. It included a solicitor (Hove), a customs officer (Farnham), a local government officer (Middlesex), a British Steel boilermaker and SDP councillor (Port Talbot), a social worker (Newcastle), two company directors (Liverpool), two trade-union officials (Ilkley and Newcastle), a dairy farmer (Norwich), a Methodist minister (Londonderry), a Labour councillor (Bristol), a director of the Commonwealth Institute (Edinburgh), a police superintendent (Essex), a Conservative councillor (Sussex), a pre-school playgroup adviser (Chorley), a chartered accountant (Gwynedd), and the vice-chairman of the Mountain Rescue Committee of Scotland.

This reform, which was directly due to the third Royal Commission's strictures about unrepresentative lay members, has secured a reasonable mix of backgrounds and geographical locations. It has, however, caused some concern to be expressed about whether new members necessarily share the council's constitutional commitment to press freedom. There is a danger that members chosen because they are 'representative' of certain groups in society will actively seek to represent the interests of these groups in a manner which may detract from the impartial adjudication of individual complaints. Shortly after her appointment one new member, Mrs Rosalie Fripp, a Labour councillor from Bristol, announced at a County Council meeting:

I'm a recently elected member of the Press Council and I'm issuing a warning to members of the press – I'm monitoring very closely the way they treat Avon County Council. The *Western Daily Press* has been extremely unfair in some of the personal attacks they have meted out on some members of the Labour Party. It's a well-known fact.[5]

These comments were reportedly delivered in the course of Mrs Fripp's support for withdrawing subscriptions to the *Western Daily Press* by County Council libraries, and they moved another local newspaper to comment: 'The threat of Mrs Fripp is only to Press Council credibility.' The Press Council reassured newspapers in her area that Mrs Fripp would not sit on any committee considering complaints against them.[6] The incident illustrates the problem, which will be a recurrent theme in this study, of the Press Council wearing two hats – defender of press freedom, and punisher of press misconduct. Mrs Fripp may be admirably qualified to contribute to the latter role, but might not the former demand criticism of local councils which refuse on political grounds to purchase particular newspapers for public libraries?

Most of the eighteen nominated press members have vested interests in newspapers which are liable to suffer council criticism. If its ethical principles are to command respect in the industry, some part in their formulation must be played by experienced editors and journalists. The council tries to avoid direct conflicts of interest by ensuring that no member participates in the adjudication of a complaint against his or her own paper. It sometimes happens, however, that a council member appears before colleagues on a complaints committee as a representative, defending his newspaper against a particular complaint. For example Mr Henry Douglas, legal manager of the *Sun* and the *News of the World*, was for many years a member of the council nominated by the Institute of Journalists. At the same time he represented his newspapers, both in person and in writing, when complaints were made against them. The council's report for 1979 records two such occasions.[7] Similarly Mr Michael Randolph, editor of the *Reader's Digest*, was a member of the council nominated by the Periodical Publishers' Association in 1978 when he twice defended his journal against criticism.[8] There is no suggestion that they took part in judging their own cases, but obviously complainants (who are not allowed legal representation) are likely to feel at a disadvantage when the case against them is argued by a member of the very body whose judgement is being sought. It is not enough for the council to insist, as it did after the Fripp incident, that 'members sit as individuals, not as representatives'. When press members act as press representatives, it is at least incumbent on the council to designate another of its members to advise and represent the complainant.

Often, the Press Council cannot avoid becoming a judge in the cause of one of its own members. In the course of its long enquiry into the behaviour of the *Daily Mail* in the Sutcliffe case, for example, the council was called upon to consider the conduct of the managing editor of that newspaper, Alwyn Robinson.[9] It was he who had given a written assurance to Mrs Hill, mother of a Sutcliffe victim, that not a penny had or would be paid by the *Mail* to the murderer's wife. His letter did not mention the negotiations which *Mail* executives had conducted with the wife's solicitors a few weeks before, mentioning five-figure sums for her story, or the detailed contract providing for monies to be paid at her direction which was drawn up by the newspaper's legal department. Nor did he mention a cash payment of £5000 made to the murderer's father. Called upon by the complaints committee to explain his letter, Mr Robinson wrote that he had known nothing of these events. He also asserted that the *Mail*'s editor decided, at an early stage, to make no payments to Mrs Sutcliffe. The Press Council committee accepted his evidence without asking him to attend for questioning. He was, at the time, a vice-chairman of the Press Council.

Many of the Press Council's organizational problems stem from the unwieldy size of its membership. Thirty-six voluntary members provide breadth at the expense of expertise and efficiency. The Swedish Press Council and the Broadcasting Complaints Commission have five members, and the ASA has twelve, three of whom are active in consumer rights organizations. Selection of 'ordinary members of the public' from a range of occupations and localities has a comforting democratic ring, but if those persons have no experience of assessing evidence and judging disputes, or of representing the public interest on consumer issues, their gifted amateurism may take the form of deference to an executive whose director is secretary of the body which appointed them. The council would certainly be stronger if it were smaller, with lay representatives nominated by bodies like the National Council for Civil Liberties, the National Consumer Council and the Legal Action Group.

Chairman and Staff

The constitution of the Press Council requires that its chairman must not be directly connected with the press. Since 1964 the chairman has been a distinguished lawyer. Lord Devlin was succeeded by another retired judge, Lord Pearce, who was followed in turn by Lord Shawcross. Since 1978 the chairman has been Patrick Neill QC, the Warden of All Souls' College and chairman of the Council for the Securities Industry. The job is part-time, although it carries a salary said to be in the order of £18,000 per year. The burden which the chairman must carry is a heavy one, and if the council is ever to be in a position to make a prompt response – for example, to order publication of a correction at a time when it can have a real effect, within days of the original publication – it may require full-time leadership.

The council has a total staff of eleven:

Director (Kenneth Morgan) who is the chief official and responsible for conduct of the council's affairs.

Assistant director (Charles White) who is responsible for dealing with complaints from the public.

Secretary (Ray Swingler) who is responsible for administration, conduct of enquiries by the council, and the handling of parliamentary matters and conciliation.

Two assistant secretaries dealing with complaints.

An assistant secretary who is membership secretary and minute-taker to the council and its committees.

An assistant secretary who deals with finance and is the office supervisor.

The director's secretary; one senior and two junior copy-typists.

The council has, in effect, only three experienced and senior full-time officials. They are highly competent, but their task is to process hundreds of complaints each year, survey the ethical performance of the British press, defend newspaper freedom, survey censorship trends and generally conduct the affairs of the council. The consequences of this understaffing will become evident in the course of this book, and it can be seen in the council's failure to produce annual reports until three years after the end of the year in question. Additional resources could, under present arrangements, only be provided by the newspaper proprietors, whose bill has risen from £4100 at the council's inception to £19,910 in 1966, £44,425 in 1975, £99,000 in 1977 and £155,744 in 1979. In 1983 it was estimated to be in the vicinity of £300,000. The council firmly opposes any approach to the government for funding, doubtless fearing the strings which might be attached, although there is no reason in principle why public money should not support a public service. Many private organizations accept public funds under arrangements which in no way compromise their independence.

The Complaints Procedure

Over 80% of the council's workload is taken up by the process of adjudicating complaints from members of the public. It publishes a four-page roneoed document to assist potential complainants. [10] All complaints received by the council are sent directly to the editor of the offending publication, and only if he or she fails to take satisfactory action will the council assume jurisdiction. The potential complainant is told that if redress is not forthcoming within a reasonable time (e.g. a fortnight) a statement of complaint ('what you think was improper, why you think it was wrong') together with relevant correspondence and statements by relevant witnesses (e.g. to an interview which has allegedly been distorted) should be forwarded to the director. The complainant is invited to try 'the conciliation procedure' – an attempt to resolve the matter swiftly and informally by agreement between the parties. But of 671 complaints in 1979, only seventeen were settled by conciliation. [11]

If conciliation fails, or is not tried, the council's staff will proceed to 'investigate'. The council has no investigators. Its work in this respect is confined to requesting each side to investigate and send it the evidence. Additionally, it often asks the complainant for 'clarification of the offence against ethical press standards'. If the complainant is able to show that there is a prima facie case of 'breaches of recognised standards of press conduct', the council will ask the editor to respond, and will then invite the complainant to respond to the editor's response. Sometimes, it will invite the editor to respond to the claimant's response, and so on.

Ultimately, the dossier is put before a meeting of the council's complaints committee. There are in fact three separate complaints committees, made up of members of the council, with lay and press members equally represented on each. The committee can halt an enquiry if it finds no case to answer. It can decide the case on the basis of the dossier, or it can order an oral hearing when both complainant and newspaper representative will be invited to attend. (The newspaper has the right, denied to the complainant, of *requiring* an oral hearing.)

The complaints committee subsequently draws up a draft report and an adjudication. This is submitted, together with minutes of any oral hearing and the dossier, to one of the two-monthly meetings of the full council. The council may send it back to the complaints committee for further evidence or consideration, or may approve it with or without alteration. When finally approved, the adjudication is sent to both parties shortly before it is released for general publication. Occasionally one of the parties objects to the terms of the 'final' adjudication, and it is withheld until the objections can be considered.

This procedure is considered in detail in the next chapter, in the light of evidence from those who have been through it. Detailed criticisms are made of the potential for delay at every stage; the onus placed upon the complainant to formulate his or her objection by reference to 'recognised standards' which the Press Council has been unable to codify; and the advantage, available to the newspaper alone, of being entitled to an oral hearing.

The Complaints Record

The figures available in relation to public complaints are as follows:[12]

Year	Complaints Received	Complaints Withdrawn delayed or	Disallowed (i.e. deemed frivolous)	Adjudicated	Upheld	% upheld in relation to number submitted	Rejected
69–79	492	394	53	45	20	4.06	25
70–71	370	267	67	38	13	3.51	25
71–72	398	299	52	47	20	5.02	27
72–73	412	324	64	34	20	4.85	14
73–74	390	282	67	41	14	3.58	27
74–75	425	296	74	55	32	7.52	23
75–76	507	353	75	79	34	6.70	45
76–77	665	480	117	68	30	4.51	38
July 77– March 80	1566	1061	309	155	73	4.66	82

In the period 1977–80 it should be added that forty-one complaints were successfully conciliated.

The council finds that British newspapers and magazines

commit, on average each year, about thirty breaches of ethical standards. This may either be viewed as a remarkable tribute to the character and conduct of the British press, or as a measure of the limited degree to which the council is able to monitor its performance. The council, of course, generally acts only when people bother to complain – it has consistently refused to engage in thorough monitoring work of the sort done in relation to newspaper advertisements by a special section of the Advertising Standards Authority. The real level of adherence to Press Council principles cannot therefore be estimated.

Another feature of this record is that the great majority of complaints are withdrawn before they are ever considered. Why so many? The director has said: 'it is not possible for the Council to say what the motivation is'.[13] In some cases, of course, it will be because the editor has offered a satisfactory explanation, or has published the desired correction or apology. The phenomenon of the high proportion of 'withdrawn complaints' could have a less comfortable explanation, namely that the council's various rules and practices pose obstacles which deter all but the most articulate or determined complainants.

Legal Waiver

Some complaints made to the Press Council could equally be made the subject of a legal action against the newspaper concerned. In such cases, the council will not proceed further unless the complainant signs a 'legal waiver' – a written undertaking to the proprietors and editor of the newspaper that in return for their agreement to cooperate with the council and to publish its adjudication: 'I hereby release you, your servants and agents from all legal claims arising out of the said complaint.'[14]

The insistence upon a legal waiver is bitterly resented by some complainants. The council's practice was considered, and criticized, by the Annan Committee on the Future of Broadcasting:

Our conclusion was that the waiver was an unjustifiable interference with individual rights. Complainants should not have to choose between public vindication or legal redress. They are entitled in some cases to both. We were sceptical about the argument of 'double jeopardy' which has been used to support the waiver, particularly in view of the likely costs of legal action. Indeed some members of the committee had doubts about the legality of the waiver in depriving citizens of their right of access to the courts.[15]

The third Royal Commission was also unimpressed by the legal waiver procedure. Some members thought it indicated that 'the Press Council is more concerned to protect newspapers from the public than to raise the standards of the newspapers in the interests of the public'. The other members acknowledged that it may have a limited justification, but recommended that the Press Council should reconsider the waiver with a view to abolishing it.[16]

The council has declined to abolish the waiver. It defends its practice on the ground that editors cannot be expected to cooperate unless assured that the evidence they provide to the council will not subsequently be used against them in court actions. It is fearful that adverse adjudications might damage a newspaper defendant in court. Without the waiver the newspaper concerned could be placed in 'double jeopardy', it told the third Royal Commission.[17]

Several points should be made in relation to the council's defence of its practice. Since the council has no legal powers, it is inappropriate to suggest that an adverse adjudication places a newspaper or its staff in 'jeopardy' in any meaningful sense. The claim that a newspaper would be inhibited in disclosing evidence which could be used in legal actions overlooks the fact that in all civil actions in this country there is a process called 'discovery', which obliges each party to disclose to the other the contents of all material in its possession or power which is relevant to issues at the trial. A plaintiff is normally entitled to see the newspaper's documentary evidence, except for material which would reveal journalistic sources.

The fear that an adverse adjudication might be used *against* a newspaper defendant in court is similarly exaggerated. It is a basic principle of the law of evidence that issues of fact are for the tribunal – the jury or judge – to decide at the trial, and any findings on those facts by another tribunal – such as the Press Council – would generally be inadmissable. However, the fact that an adverse adjudication has been made and published could be helpful to the newspaper by reducing its liability to pay damages if it lost a libel action; the fact that the plaintiff's reputation had already been publicly vindicated, and that vindication published by the defendant, would considerably reduce the damages which would otherwise be awarded.

It follows that the occasions when a newspaper might reasonably be expected to be prejudiced in subsequent legal proceedings by Press Council action are where the substance of the complaint could be made the subject of a criminal prosecution, or where the justification of its conduct would involve the revelation of a source. The newspaper might be prepared to reveal its source in confidence to the council, but not in public to a court. In these limited classes of case, the waiver is justified.

The principal objection to the 'legal waiver' is that questions of legal liability are irrelevant to the task of maintaining professional standards. The role of the Press Council is to adjudicate the question of whether standards have been breached in particular cases, and not to exact any punishment or financial compensation for the consequences of that breach. For example, an editor may commit plagiarism or publish a freelance contribution without acknowledgement or payment. His or her conduct may be attended by the most flagrant dishonesty towards the contributor and the reading public. The role of the law is to compensate the victim for breach of copyright and breach of contract. The legal action may be settled out of court, or may go unreported. The role of the Press Council *should* be publicly to condemn the editor for gross breaches of professional standards, and to oblige him or her to publish its findings prominently. Its insistence on a legal waiver in cases which do not involve allegations of crime or revelation of sources is usually unnecessary.

The Annan Committee had doubts about the extent to which the legal waiver is legally valid. Some agreements purporting to oust entirely the jurisdiction of the courts have been held void on grounds of public policy. There would be no objection to parties in a dispute agreeing to accept the Press Council's arbitration of that dispute as an alternative to a court of law but, as we have seen, the legal issues involved in libel, contract and copyright may be quite separate and distinct from the question of whether professional standards have been breached. In 1982 the Law Lords stressed the importance of the principle of uninhibited access to the courts: 'The principle has been strongly affirmed by the European Court of Human Rights in the [Golder] case. The court there decided that access to a court was a right protected by Article 6 of the European Convention on the Protection of Human Rights and Fundamental Freedoms . . .'[18]

Article 6 of the European Convention provides that in the determination of his or her civil rights every citizen is entitled to a fair and public hearing by an independent and impartial tribunal established by law. The right to reputation is a civil right: the Press Council does not give a public hearing, and is not a tribunal established by law. It would be unconscionable if a court were to debar a plaintiff from recovering money due and owing, or from obtaining compensation for plagiarism, simply because the Press Council had been asked to criticize the ethics (as distinct from the legalities) of an editor's behaviour. The council makes no mention of the complexities of the legal position, either in the waiver form itself or in its 'Guidance on Procedure for Complainants'.

The Council and the Courts

The Press Council has an uneasy status in disputes between people and the press. It lacks the powers of a court, or the contractual commitments which safeguard the position of an arbitrator, yet it hears evidence and then records a judgement which purports to settle a grievance between two opposing parties. As a private tribunal it is not bound by law to obey the rules of natural justice, and no appeal lies from its findings to any higher court. It serves the interests of the newspaper proprietors who fund it, because it provides an outlet for some public complaints which might otherwise result in legal action, and its claims to be a regulatory agency are used to forestall the establishment of a tribunal with legal 'teeth'. Many of the complaints it adjudicates involve questions of individual reputation which could equally be made the subject of an action for libel; in such cases it operates as an alternative to the courts. Its lack of powers to award compensation or damages, or even to guarantee the publication of its adjudications, makes it a poor alternative, but since legal aid is unavailable for libel, it functions in effect as a poor person's libel court.

As a private body, it has no power to protect those who elect to use its services from reprisals from the newspapers they complain against. Examples of successful complainants who have been derided and condemned by unrepentant editors are given in Chapter 4 (see p.64). More seriously, however, it cannot even stop editors from threatening to sue members of the public who complain to the council. One striking example occurred in 1977, when a member of the public made a complaint to the Press Council about his local newspaper, and informed the editor, in a rather angry letter, that he had done so. The editor's response was to write back to him: 'I am advising [the reporter] to take action against you for again accusing her of malice. I am sending a copy of this letter to the Press Council.' If members of the public are to have any confidence in the council, they must not be afraid that their complaints against the press will provoke a libel action against them by an offended editor or reporter. It might be expected that the council would recognize this fundamental danger to its position, and would act immediately to discourage legal action against its complainant. Instead, it gave credence to the editor's threat by replying: 'The Press Council will take no further action in this matter until any threatened proceedings have been disposed of. . . .'[19]

The Press Council's supine attitude in this case suggests that newspapers, editors or reporters could avoid its adjudicative procedures simply by threatening libel actions against complainants. Such actions would in most cases be doomed to failure, because in libel law an individual has 'qualified privilege' both to respond in a defamatory manner to an attack on his or her probity, and to report misbehaviour to an organization which might reasonably be thought capable of correcting it. This privilege protects statements, even if inaccurate or exaggerated, unless the author knows they are false. But complainants cannot be expected to know the finer points of libel law. The Press Council must find some way of reassuring members of the public – on whom, after all, it depends for evidence of breaches of press standards – that they will suffer no harm by complaining to the council.

Publicity

The complaints committee sits in secret, even when both parties attend to give evidence. Notes of evidence are taken, but no transcript is produced. This is contrary to the practice of its American equivalent, the National News Council, whose 'grievance committee' holds its hearings in public. There are obviously some complaints, relating to invasion of privacy, where publicity which would further identify the complainant would be counter-productive, and in such cases the council issues its adjudication privately to the parties and subsequently reports it in such a way as to preserve anonymity. But there are many cases involving ethical principles where the form and presentation of the opposing sides' arguments are matters of real public interest. It would have been most illuminating, for example, to hear editors defend in public their payments of blood money in the Sutcliffe case under close questioning. Those criticized by the council all refused to appear on television, when the report was published, to defend their actions. Opening the complaints committee sessions to the press would take important debates into a wider arena, and make the council's judgements, when delivered, better understood and appreciated. It is anomalous, to say the least, that an organization which has condemned local authorities and other bodies for excluding reporters from committee meetings should always hold its own behind closed doors.

The council defends the secrecy of its committee hearings on the basis that this protects speakers from legal action for defamatory statements. It is true that the 1952 Defamation Act, which extends 'qualified privilege' to protect reports of comments made on most public occasions, does not include Press Council meetings or adjudications in its terms, although it is likely that the courts, if ever they were asked, would extend the common law doctrine to provide this protection. In any event, discussions of ethical principles should not in most cases run any risk. A more practical objection to affording open justice is simply that the council's building in Salisbury Square does not have suitable accommodation for public hearings. This objection could easily be met by hiring an appropriate venue.

Council adjudications are issued as press releases, with publication embargoed for five days – a time thought sufficient to allow parties to point out any errors of fact. The press, including the offending newspaper, is in no way *bound* to publish the adjudication, or any part of it, unless of course the editor has agreed to do so in return for a waiver of the complainant's legal rights. In practice, most newspapers found in default, and all newspapers whose actions have been vindicated, give some publicity to the adjudication. The publicity given to an adverse adjudication is often not commensurate with the prominence originally given to the offending article. Frequently the adjudication is summarized, and there have been occasions when the report of the adjudication has been distorted. Reports of council adjudications are often carried in the national press, at least if they fulfil the criterion of 'newsworthiness' (i.e. if celebrities are involved or rival papers are condemned). The only regular and full account of adjudications is to be found in a special column of the *UK Press Gazette* – a publication for the press trade – and in the Press Council's Annual Report, which has become a retrospective account of its actions published several years later.

A Code of Conduct?

Neither complainants nor members of the council receive any

guide to the 'case law' which the council has built up over its thirty years of operation. There have been three major 'Declarations of Principle' – on privacy, cheque-book journalism, and the right of the press to be politically partisan – but in 1981 the council vigorously rejected the third Royal Commission's recommendation that it should 'draw up a code of behaviour on which to base its adjudications, which should set out in some detail the spirit which should govern the conduct of editors and journalists'.[20] The council claims that a code would take the form either of 'moralising platitudes' or 'a complicated mass of rules and sub-rules, subject to exceptions and provisos'.[21] Ever since its evidence to the third Royal Commission, given in 1975, it has promised from time to time that a 'résumé' of its decisions is to be published. The council's 1978 report noted that 'it is preparing a résumé of the very large number of individual decisions which the Council has made since its formation'.[22] It told the Industry and Trade Committee of the House of Commons in April 1980 that 'it does intend to go ahead with its proposal to issue on a running basis a codification of its own decisions making clear the principles which emerge from them'.[23] A similar statement of intent was 'achieved' by negotiations with the media committee of the Trade Union Congress, and announced with some fanfare in August 1982. But the last published attempt to subsume council decisions under general principles was made by H. Phillip Levy in 1967. No résumé or codification had emerged by April 1983, despite the council's promises over the years.

Other Activities

The Press Council constantly warns of the dangers of statutory regulation of British newspapers. From time to time, when particularly serious examples of media misbehaviour are condemned by judges or senior politicians, the council seeks to defuse the clamour for legislation by instituting its own enquiry. Its most ambitious effort in this direction is its report on 'Press Conduct in the Sutcliffe Case', which occupied one of its complaints committees for almost two years.[24] Seven newspapers were censured for breaking the Declaration of Principle on cheque-book journalism. These breaches came only a year after similar breaches had been the subject of an enquiry into press conduct in respect of the trial of Liberal Party leader Jeremy Thorpe.[25] In 1973 the council conducted its own enquiry into the press and Lord Lambton, the government minister, who was forced to resign after newspapers bought and published details of his interest in prostitutes and cannabis.[26] Although such enquiries are infrequent, they must be conducted if the council is to reassure parliament that voluntary regulation works better than law. Ironically the Sutcliffe enquiry produced evidence, both in the report itself and in the press reaction to it, that no amount of voluntary regulation will deter press payments to witnesses and to criminal associates in return for circulation-building scoops.

The council from time to time issues short press statements on political or legal issues affecting the press. It has taken to announcing its position by no more than a letter from its director to *The Times*. It has made submissions to government committees considering, for example, privacy and defamation, to the Law Commission and the Monopolies Commission, to the Home Office and to various professional bodies. In recent years, these submissions have not been published. In its Annual Reports it publishes statistics on newspaper holdings and circulations, and occasional papers on the state of the medium. The value of these compilations is much reduced by the fact that they currently appear three to four years after the period surveyed. It receives numerous overseas visitors, and encourages the establishment of Press Councils, along its own lines, in other countries.

The Press Council is satisfied with its work. Its former director, Noel S. Paul, explained to the Columbia Journalism Review that the council's future was secure. 'I think it has won acceptance generally, both in the esteem of the public and of the press. There will always be ample work to be done. The press always will be under some sort of pressure which requires the constant watchfulness of a body such as the Press Council.'[27] The nature of that pressure was spelled out by its present director, Kenneth Morgan: 'Its inauguration, at the instance of the first Royal Commission on the Press, and its continued existence probably have forestalled statutory controls being imposed upon the Press – a point about which the Press Council is unrepentant.'[28] The next two chapters set out evidence which suggests that the continued existence of the Press Council in its present form may produce the very statutory controls its director is proud to have averted.

3
Public Complaints

As laid down in its constitution, the objects of the council include:

> *(ii)* To maintain the character of the British Press in accordance with the highest professional and commercial standards.
>
> *(iii)* To consider complaints about the conduct of the Press or the conduct of persons and organisations towards the Press; to deal with these complaints in whatever manner might seem practical and appropriate and record resultant action.

Adjudicating public complaints is the council's most important and most time-consuming function. Upon its effectiveness depends the case against further legal controls on the press. It follows that its performance of this function is of crucial importance, both to the public, who wish to be assured that complaints are fairly and speedily adjudicated, and to the press, which relies upon that public confidence as a defence against proposals which would limit its freedom.

The complainant is crucial to the whole exercise, because the council depends almost entirely on members of the public to bring breaches of press standards to its attention. Its former director has admitted:

> The Council is free to institute its own complaints or inquiries and will do so in appropriate circumstances but it has never envisaged it as part of its duty to monitor the conduct of the Press from day to day . . . it is in the first instance the public rather than the Press Council that must establish [acceptable] standards. . . .[1]

The council places this burden upon interested members of the public, yet reserves to itself the role of maintaining the character of the British press 'in accordance with the highest professional standards'. It follows that its role can only be performed if members of the public are encouraged to come forward with their complaints. If those complaints are upheld, the newspaper is censured and the press is warned. Many complaints which turn out to be unjustified are none the less valuable: in providing reasons for dismissal the council is given the opportunity to explain to the public why the press must resort to the actions complained of, and to establish ethical guidelines. This chapter examines the level of satisfaction felt by complainants, both successful and unsuccessful, who have played the part allotted to them by the council in the task of establishing acceptable standards.

The Press Council's Claims

The Press Council has repeatedly made fulsome claims for the speed and effectiveness of its complaints machinery. For example, in an emergency public statement in 1977, repeated in 1982, it offered an assurance to the public that

. . . prompt and impartial consideration will be given by the Press Council to any complaint made by individuals, chapels or unions. The investigation of such complaints is carried out by the Council's Complaints Committee. A statement issued by the Press Council following such an inquiry receives wide publicity in the newspaper concerned and elsewhere. The terms of the statement are much more than an expression of opinion upon the conduct of the newspaper. They are specifically designed to achieve reparation by correcting inaccuracies and, in appropriate cases, providing the right of reply by the quotation of the complainant's response to the disputed publication, backed by the Council's declaration of the complainant's right to have that reply published in the offending newspaper or periodical.[2]

In its evidence to the third Royal Commission, the council stated its belief that

in general terms the system it employs for the reception,

investigation, examination and adjudication of complaints offers a fair and effective answer to the need and embraces a degree of flexibility which enables it at short notice to take account of responsible criticisms of its procedures and constructive suggestions for the benefit of the public and the media. It has the further advantage of being expeditious, wholly inexpensive to the complainants and characterised by an absence of the bureaucratic limitations which would inevitably arise in the case of a more formal body with statutory powers.

In other sections of its evidence, it asserted that 'the Secretariat takes a special pride in prompt response to communications', that 'most complaints are dealt with within three months, many in substantially less time and some take longer', and that 'it is an important feature of the Council that it offers a comparatively swift remedy to the complainant'. It also asserted:

The Press Council has thoroughly established the principle that where a person or organisation has been attacked in the columns of a newspaper they are entitled to space for a reasonable reply. Where such entitlement has been denied and a complaint to the Council is upheld, the Press Release issued for publication invariably effects the original purpose of the complainant by including the essence at least of the rejoinder.[3]

A Consumer Survey

These claims have never been properly tested, although they are fundamental to the main purpose of the Press Council. It is surprising that the council has for so long assumed a consumer satisfaction with its complaints service, without taking meaningful steps to follow up its adjudications with any study of their reception either by complainants or by the newspapers complained against. In order to investigate the practical experiences and reactions of those who had used the complaints machinery, almost a hundred persons and organizations who had been parties to Press Council adjudications since 1977 were contacted and asked for their comments. These complainants were not specially selected: they simply happened to be those whose addresses were published in, or discoverable from, reports of adjudications published in the *UK Press Gazette*.

In the event seventy-seven complainants, forty-five of whom had complaints upheld by the council, responded in detail, many supplying documentation to justify the criticisms they made of the procedure which ultimately vindicated them. This was a significant response, when it is recalled that the average number of successful complaints each year, between 1970 and 1981, has been twenty-four.

Critics of the Press Council came from all political camps and social classes. In terms of the political parties, criticism was volunteered by Conservative MP Tony Marlow, from Labour MPs Peter Snape, Frank Field, Eric Moonman and Hugh Macartney and from Liberal MP Richard Wainwright. The Secretary-General of the Liberal Party said that, after the experience of several recent complaints, 'we have come to the conclusion that the Press Council has become a pathetic white-wash body, and we have not bothered with it since'.

Other successful respondents were so dissatisfied with the Press Council that they said they would not rely upon it again. Many of them pointed out that such success as they enjoyed came only after a persistence, determination, expenditure and access to skill and resources which would not have been possible had they been less powerful or articulate. Certain criticisms of the council's attitudes, procedure and impact were made by complainant after complainant. A remarkable picture emerged of a complaints commission whose procedures seemed to give more cause for complaint than the conduct of the newspapers it was investigating.

Among the most common complaints were:

● There was excessive delay between lodging the complaint and receiving the adjudication. Contrary to the Press Council's evidence to the Royal Commission, delays of between eight and twelve months were common. The consequence of this delay, of course, was that the adjudication provided little satisfaction to the complainant. Newspaper readers had forgotten what the article was about in the first place.

● Excessive obstacles were placed in the way of complainants at the outset. Too much emphasis was placed on the need for complainants to 'formulate' a breach of good press practice, and insufficient assistance was given in arriving at such a formulation.

● The council staff were unhelpful in gathering evidence: the onus was placed on the complainant, at his or her own expense, to do all the 'investigation' necessary to prove inaccuracy or unethical conduct.

- The council tended to act as a post-box, passing letters back and forth between complainant and editor. There was little use of the telephone, and the council did not have the facilities to embark upon any investigative work itself.
- The 'legal waiver' is objectionable in principle and was a deterrent in practice.
- There was no assistance to cover expenses, such as photo-copying and travelling to obtain witness statements, even for successful complainants.
- The complainant has no right to demand an oral hearing before the complaints commission. Such a right is given, however, to the editor complained against.
- If an oral hearing was granted, the complainant was obliged to be his or her own advocate.
- The adversarial procedure adopted by the council, which requires the complainant alone to meet every point raised against the complaint prior to adjudication, ensures that only those complainants with a high level of skill and determination will be successful. The adversary system handicaps the poor or inarticulate complainant.
- When the adjudication was formulated, insufficient time was given to the parties to comment on or correct it before its release to the press.
- The offending newspaper is not bound to publish an adjudication; when it did so, it rarely gave the same prominence as the original article complained against.
- There is no safeguard against the offending newspaper distorting the adjudication, either by publishing it in part only or by carrying it under a misleading headline.
- In several cases, the newspaper whose conduct had been condemned by the council has publicly rejected the adjudication and heaped abuse on the complainant. This has been achieved by front-page editorials, and by re-statements of 'unsuccessful' defences. The Press Council is powerless to protect its complainants against such consequences.

These criticisms recurred in the evidence submitted by those forty-five respondents whose complaints had been upheld. In some cases their criticisms were supported by documentation, in others by recollections of a recent experience which obviously still loomed large in the memory of the people it most affected. The Press Council refused to discuss the conclusions drawn from this survey, so it has not been possible to check every assertion made by the successful respondents. The most significant fact, however, is that these dissatisfactions with the council have been expressed by the great majority of those who should be its most satisfied customers. The flavour of their responses is embodied in the following representative selections.

Peter Snape MP v Midland Chronicle[4] Mr Snape, the Labour MP for West Bromwich, complained that several hundred of his constituents who lived on a local estate had been branded as prostitutes, pornographers and wife-swappers in a sensationalized and inaccurate article in their local paper. This complaint was fully, indeed resoundingly, upheld. The Press Council, in one of its most uncompromising adjudications, inflicted the 'severest censure' on the newspaper. It found, on the basis of admissions by the editor, that the article was 'totally inadequately researched' and was 'a deplorable example of sensationalised journalism of a kind likely to bring the British Press into disrepute'. This adjudication is among the strongest ever issued by the Press Council, and one would expect that if anyone was satisfied with its performance, it would be Mr Snape. On the contrary, he said that he was 'largely dissatisfied' with his experience of the council, and 'would be fairly unwilling to go through the whole business again'.[5] Among his reasons for this attitude were:

● The 'long delay' (over nine months) before the actual hearing, and a further delay of six weeks before the decision was announced.

● The obstruction and delay occasioned by the council's formulation of the complaint. 'There was an initial exchange of three letters with the complaints secretary who asked repeatedly on what basis the complaint was being made. Subsequently, some considerable time was spent in outlining the substance of the complaint prior to the hearing, although I should have thought that the reason was glaringly obvious.'

● The upheld complaint was not given a prominence comparable to the original distortion. 'The offending newspaper placed the decision on an inside page, although the original story had been a front-page lead.'

The residents of the estate were fortunate in having Peter Snape as their advocate: his experience and resources enabled him to collect the evidence and pursue the complaint to a 'successful' conclusion. Most victims of press misconduct are not so fortunate. It is interesting to note, in relation to the claim that council adjudications are respected and obeyed, that only two years later the council was obliged to censure another local newspaper, this time the *Tamworth Herald,* which had an almost identical story about 'sex games' on a council estate. Once again, a newspaper had 'painted an exaggerated picture on flimsy evidence'. Once again, it fell to a local MP, Bruce Grocott, to defend the morals of his constituents against the bogus prying of their local paper.

Paul Francis v Belper News[6] The Press Council held that a local newspaper had, on three separate matters, inaccurately reported a political controversy over secondary education. Although the mistakes were found not to have been deliberate, one report had given a 'misleading and false impression', another had been misleading and unfair to a headmaster, and 'careless sub-editing' had given a 'tendentious impression'. All those errors had tended to support the political campaign of the chairman of the newspaper's proprietors, who was standing for a local election, and an advertisement for his campaign had been published on the same page as one of the misleadingly supportive reports. The council's adjudication was therefore a valuable objective view of a passionate and partisan local issue and a necessary corrective to a number of inaccurate reports. One would expect the successful complainant, Paul Francis, to be well satisfied that his personal initiative had been vindicated, especially since any adverse finding could have reflected on the record of the school he wished to defend.

But Mr Francis regards the Press Council's adjudication as 'a belated crumb of comfort'. It took eleven months from the time he complained to the release of the council's decision. Consequently, 'a lot of the damage had already been done' and 'in terms of impact, the actual occasion was hardly noticed . . . the local radio station, which had been eager to know more when the temperature was higher, lost interest by the time the case had been judged'. This case is a classic example of the public interest demanding a speedy investigation and rectification of press inaccuracies which might have affected voting at an election. The delay of eleven months seems indefensible.

Paul Francis was not an MP, nor was he personally involved in the inaccuracies. He was a teacher at the school. He comments that 'I needed to have an eccentric mixture of commitment, articulacy, energy and rage to go through the whole process at all. I spent a lot of time and covered a lot of paper in the course of my submission, which . . . does suggest that the Press Council is not going to be directly useful to a large proportion of the population.'[7]

Dorothy Harwood v Sunday Independent[8] The Torbay Operatic and Dramatic Society mounted a children's production of *Guys and Dolls*. The local Sunday newspaper devoted its front page to 'Storm over Teeny Strip' – a storm contrived by the newspaper itself. The Press Council found that the story was exaggerated, the headline was objectionable, and the whole piece was editorial opinion disguised as news. This decision was reached after considering evidence from a number of people quoted in the article, such evidence being collected by the complainant at the request of the council, which told her that 'The Press Council does not assemble evidence on behalf of complainants.'[9] The story was damaging to the society's producer, Mrs Harwood, by implying that she was engaging young children to perform erotic scenes attractive to perverts, and the newspaper, which had 'sought to create a storm where none existed', was perhaps fortunate that she lacked the funds and the support (her husband was dying of cancer) to bring a libel suit against it. In this class of case the Press Council functions in effect as an alternative to the libel laws, and it extracted the customary 'legal waiver' before it would consider the complaint.

Dorothy Harwood, although vindicated by the adjudication, was dissatisfied on a number of scores. It took ten months for the Press Council to adjudicate the complaint. In collecting the evidence, photostating it, and attending with witnesses at an oral hearing in London, she had been put to considerable expense, for which she was not compensated despite the fact that her complaint was upheld. The Press Council's adjudication was carried by the offending newspaper, but it was buried on an inside page, whereas the original story had occupied almost the entire front page. She never received an apology from the editor, nor was an apology printed in the paper. Finally, she pinpoints an important inadequacy in the council's claim to impose a 'moral obligation' on offending newspapers to publish its decision. This story was given such a sensational treatment in the local paper that it was picked up and published in shortened form in many national newspapers. Those national papers were under no 'moral obligation' to publish the Press Council's corrective, since they were not at fault, and most did not in fact publish it.[10]

Shelter v Daily Express[11] The Press Council held that the *Daily*

Express published a front-page splash story that was misleading and harmful, wrongfully implying that a mother and her three children had jumped the housing queue. Not only did it fail to correct the errors in the story, but it published three readers' letters repeating the facts which by then it should have known to be untrue, thereby prolonging the misleading impression given to its readers. The mother was subjected to abusive letters and further hostile comment in her local press, and her case was taken to the Press Council by Shelter, the National Campaign for the Homeless. The Press Council's judgement was a serious indictment of the conduct of a national newspaper, yet Shelter officials are highly critical of the council's performance.[12] They point out:

(i) The complaint took over ten months to adjudicate. The errors of fact were simple to establish, and the delay prolonged the distress that their original publication caused to the mother. The inaccuracies were of a kind to encourage personal abuse and difficulties with neighbours, and they called for urgent rectification.

(ii) The council delayed putting its complaints machinery in motion. The correspondence between Shelter and the Press Council shows that the council persistently refused, for six weeks, to accept the complaint until it was satisfied that the editor had closed his private correspondence with Shelter. Since it was apparent from the outset that part of the complaint was that the newspaper had published readers' letters at a time when it knew that they contained incorrect statements, the council's reason for delay was disingenuous. The council's practice in this respect means that an editor could delay a complaint, simply by asking the complainant repeatedly for further information.

(iii) The *Express* published the council's adjudication on page four, but without any apology to the mother it had humiliated. Local papers, which had reported the *Express* story, did not feel it necessary to report the adjudication at all.

Other Successful Complainants

The concerns illustrated in the above four examples are echoed by many other successful complainants:

● Michael Moulder, author of the *The Shell Guide to Shropshire,* had some of his work reproduced in the *Observer* without adequate acknowledgement.[13] His satisfaction at the adjudication was 'considerably diminished' by the delay (ten months) which made it 'inevitable that it would make little or no impact on the readers of the original article. In my view, this defeated the whole purpose of my complaint.' Redress from the Press Council was sought as an alternative to legal action over copyright, and he was understandably critical of the 'legal waiver'.

● Soccer referee Ken Aston was the victim of a misleading headline and commentary in the *Daily Express*. The delay (six months) 'tends to devalue the whole process'. He received no compensation for expenses incurred in laying his complaint, obtained no apology from the newspaper, and regards the legal waiver as amounting 'almost to a limitation of human rights'.[14]

● Television producer Leslie Woodhead was the victim of what the Press Council condemned as 'a glaring example of improper journalism by innuendo' – a scurrilous and unfounded piece of gossip in the *Daily Mail* which caused distress to his family. Although appreciative of the council's thoroughness, 'I would have wished for a speedier adjudication so as to lessen the tension for my family . . . for a complainant a wait of more than seven months can seem interminable while the damaging report remains on the record'. He is also concerned about the legal waiver: 'It does seem a stiff penalty to have to trade all rights to damages in order to secure the correction of a distorted and harmful report.' He adds, and it is an important point which will be considered in Chapter 5, 'I would like to hear the Council speaking out more clearly and frequently against encroachments on press freedom.'[15]

● Graeme Kidd, editor of the Aston University student newspaper, successfully complained that the Birmingham *Evening Mail* had published a misleading account of a lecture at the university and had unfairly misrepresented the position of the president of the Student's Guild. He points out that the thirteen-month delay between the appearance of the article and the appearance of the council adjudication 'must surely have rendered the value of any corrections or redress rather insignificant'.[16]

● Ralph Glasser's complaint about a cartoon in the *Evening Standard* was upheld by the Press Council in the strongest terms. (The cartoon depicted a butler striking an old man on the head with a spade, in an apparent reference to a current murder case.) It condemned the cartoon as 'a shocking outrage on decency and justice relating to a case of the utmost gravity which was then still proceeding in the courts and calculated not only to cause distress to relatives and friends of [the murdered man] but also to outrage the public'.[17] Despite this success, Mr Glasser was nonetheless critical of the council's procedures after it had received his complaint:

> The Council at first confined itself to acting as a post office and nothing more. It forwarded my letter to the Editor and told me that it would take no further action unless I was dissatisfied with the reply – or no reply – that I received. If so I should write again. Now this purely passive behaviour seems strange, to say the least, for a body presenting itself as 'investigating complaints against newspapers' – but perhaps not in a body mainly representing the press itself. And one assumes, too, from this placing of the onus on the outside complainer, *and* on his persistence in his complaint, that the Council will tend not to act on its own to preserve standards of behaviour. The Council, if it accepts its alleged function, should commit itself to do two things:
> *(a)* take a view of what constitutes the public interest;
> *(b)* be willing to involve itself immediately in protecting that interest.
> Simply to hold the ring and forward letters unless pressed to do more is to adopt a weak and supine position, far from that of a watchdog. A watchdog that has to be forced to be aggressive is not a watchdog.[18]

● Dr Violet Rowe successfully complained about the racist slant of a headline in the *Sunday People*. She feels that the months of delay in dealing with her complaint ensured that 'readers would have forgotten what was in it. So I had wasted my time.' She was indignant at the newspaper's refusal to apologize, and felt that there should have been at least one black person on the council's complaints committee.[19]

● Tony Smythe is the National Director of MIND, an organization which has twice successfully represented patients and staff at mental hospitals in complaints to the Press Council:

> I cannot over-emphasize the enormous amount of work that was involved . . . . None of our expenses were paid although we requested them (witnesses had to travel from Lancashire to attend the hearings) and we were not allowed any legal representative which would have saved my time at least . . . .

I honestly do not believe that the people making the complaint would have succeeded without my representation and I would go on from that to question what chances an ordinary citizen acting on his or her own behalf would have without the backing of the secretarial facilities which are available to me.[20]

• Kenneth Grant was the father of a union chapel whose actions had been criticized in the *New Statesman*. The council censured that journal for refusing to publish his letter of reply, even in an abridged form. He lives in Edinburgh, and the complaint involved him in considerable financial outlay at a time when he was unemployed. His dissatisfaction with the whole procedure was such that he wrote to the council informing it that he would never make another complaint.[21]

• Miner's leader Arthur Scargill, now in his forties and a prominent member of the Labour Party, was a member of the Young Communist League between the ages of sixteen and twenty-one. The Press Council held that the *News of the World* had made a damaging error in describing him as 'the Yorkshire Communist', and was wrong to refuse to print an appropriate correction. Mr Scargill was critical both of the council's delay and of the contempt which the newspaper showed for the Press Council by re-asserting its case at the same time as it published the adjudication. As a seasoned complainer to the council, he emphasizes the importance of an oral hearing, and believes that complainants should have a right to demand one. He argues for a council with legal powers to order offending papers to carry adjudications and apologies, and to fine them if they disobey.[22]

• The former chief executive of Wakefield Council succeeded in a complaint that the local newspaper had failed to publish 'an adequate and timely correction' to a story about a proposed council service. This adjudication came eight months after the complaint was lodged, and was not given the same prominence by the newspaper as the original story. The present chief executive considers that the Press Council's response, like that of the newspaper it criticized, was neither 'adequate or timely'. He comments that 'The lack of effective redress against press distortion is an obstacle to good relationships between councils and local newspapers . . . our experience with the Press Council led us to believe that their function seemed to be to vindicate the press action rather than to criticize.'[23]

• Dorothy Smythe suffered embarrassment when a *Guardian* columnist took what the Press Council described as a 'totally unjustified and reprehensible' decision to publish her surname, although particularly asked not to, when using an extract from a letter written to the column. Mrs Smythe feels that the Press Council's procedures would have deterred a less determined complainant, that the legal waiver put unnecessary pressure on her, that the investigation, although fair, took over six 'ponderous' months, and that the published adjudication was subjected to ridicule by the columnist. 'It was, in fact, a pretty hollow victory.'[24]

• Norman Welch was the victim of what the Press Council termed 'a deplorable personal attack which goes beyond the bounds of the acceptable standards of journalism' in his local newspaper. He was advised by counsel that he had a good case against the newspaper for defamation, but he was deterred by the expense and so sought the assistance of the Press Council. He is critical of the 'legal waiver', of the council's dilatory procedures (he suggests that it should impose strict time limits), the lack of prominence given by the newspaper to the adjudication, and the lack of any effective sanction against the journalist found to be at fault.[25]

• Lady Colin Campbell was 'rather dissatisfied' with the procedure which took a year to uphold her complaint. She argued for stricter time limits for newspaper responses, a maximum period of two months from complaint to adjudication, and a more objective and representative 'jury' to decide disputed questions of fact.[26]

• The head of publicity for the National Theatre echoed a number of complaints in noticing the potential for unfair reporting which arises when complaints against an article are made on more than one ground. The council may uphold the major criticism, although dismiss others. Yet the very fact that one ground of complaint has been rejected permits the offending newspaper to headline the rejection, and to report the case as a 'victory', while playing down the real significance of the adjudication, namely that the newspaper has been held to have offended against an ethical standard.[27]

• Jeff Pirie, whose complaint led the Press Council to condemn the editor of the *Sunday Express* for a 'totally unjustifiable' publication which could 'stir up racialism', found that the publication of his address in résumés of the adjudication made him the victim of abusive and threatening letters.[28] (Mr. E.F. Earwaker, an unsuccessful complainant, said that he too received crank telephone calls as a result of the adjudication.)[29]

Since the editor of the *Sunday Express* immediately re-published the story which was the basis of the complaint, accompanied by resounding abuse of the Press Council, Mr Pirie may well feel that individuals have more to lose than gain by making complaints. His experience supports the view that the council should itself investigate breaches of standards which are drawn to its attention by members of the public who have no direct personal involvement in the subject-matter of the story.

● Further support for this approach is provided by the example of Penelope Money-Coutts, who drew the council's attention to the publication of a photograph which was in clear breach of its own guidelines on privacy. She had 'absolutely no idea that I would have to act as my own advocate – I thought a complaint was then looked into by those much wiser and more lucid than me. I felt awful when I realized what I had to do, but soon warmed to the subject.'[30] The success of her complaint is a tribute to individuals who do take up important matters which do not affect them personally, but it does detract from the council's boast to maintain the highest standards of the profession if those standards are only enforced at the occasional insistence of public-spirited individuals.

● Mary Littledale, another individual in this category, was 'somewhat dissatisfied' that the council took nine months to correct a glaring inaccuracy in a purportedly factual report on aircraft noise, especially as she had dropped part of her complaint in a vain attempt to speed up the adjudication.[31]

● The chairman of Sefton Area Health Authority,[32] and the publicity officers of both Harrow[33] and Derbyshire Councils,[34] were all concerned that the length of time (in the latter case, almost a year) negated the impact of the adjudication. This view is shared by the secretary of the Golders Green Unitarian Church, whose dissatisfaction led him to form an impression common among complainants, namely that 'the Press Council is more concerned in defending the press than in defending people against inaccurate and damaging reporting'.[35]

● Even those few successful complainants who said they were satisfied with the council's approach to its task were critical of procedural delay. As the ex-editor of the *Eton Chronicle,* who had complained about misrepresentation in the William Hickey column, put it, 'I was asked three or four times to supply details which should have been requested before, and so far as I recall the adjudication came some six months after my original complaint – long enough to ensure that not a single *Express* reader remembered the item about which the complaint was made'.[36]

Correspondence and comments were received from forty-five persons and organizations whose complaints were fully or partly upheld by the council between 1977 and 1981. Only four of the successful respondents expressed full satisfaction with the Press Council. In addition to the matters indicated above, a significant number commented adversely on the Press Council's lack of any enforceable sanction against offending (or even persistently offending) newspapers and journalists, and many felt that, even though their action had been vindicated, the council had nonetheless appeared to them to favour the press in its handling of the complaints. A number of complainants expressed cynicism about the council's claim to have conducted 'enquiries'. They point out that it has no investigative team, and the only enquiries it conducts are postal requests to both parties to supply further information. Several were particularly scathing about the council's reluctance to use the telephone to speed up its procedures.

The Unsuccessful Complainants

The thirty-two respondents whose complaints were rejected might be thought to have some axe to grind, but it is significant that their concerns for the most part emphasize and endorse the criticisms made by successful complainants. In some cases, their experience provides additional insights into the ways in which the council's consumers develop hostility towards the service it provides. For example:

Delay Concern over the delay in adjudicating complaints was similar to that found amongst successful complainants. For example: C.I. Boswell (ten months); Frank Field MP (twelve months); Richard Wainwright MP (an 'unforgiveable delay' of four and a half months); the Naturist Foundation (fourteen months); R.J. Pritchard (thirteen months); R.J. Sealey (five and a half months before the council informed Mr Sealey that his complaint was inadmissible, and redirected him to the Advertising Standards Authority); the Liberal Party (fifteen months); Sappho (eight months); W.J. Taylor (ten months). The frustration of these complainants is expressed by Mr Taylor:

My view of this experience is that no attempt is made to deal with topical matters quickly: even had my complaint been upheld the passage of several months would have made the judgement of little interest – for many months the impressions left by the original report would have seemingly gone unchallenged, and there seemed to be no attempt to deal with anything urgently. I allege that the whole conduct of the affair was such that it did seem that the hope was that sufficient delay would cause me to drop the complaint, and I consider I was put to inordinate trouble in a matter which could have been dealt with within a week. The to and fro tactics with the editor seemed to me to have no justification: either the article as printed was open to my stated complaint or it wasn't – a matter which could have been decided without the elaborate procedure adopted. I draw the conclusion that the Press Council may be disregarded as a serious body. The method was too slow; trivial technicalities were introduced whenever possible; it took three different people holding down four different jobs to deal with the correspondence to me alone . . . . A more sensitive person than myself might well have got the feeling that he was the one under complaint in the early stages; a less persistent complainer might well have given it all up.[37]

Right to a hearing Frank Field MP submitted a complete dossier of his correspondence with the Press Council over an article which was found to contain an inaccuracy, albeit not one which was 'unfair or damaging'.[38] Mr Field asserted that his complaint was adjudicated by a 'kangaroo court', which gave him no opportunity to present his case in person. It is clear that from the inception of his complaint he expected to be accorded an oral hearing, and that he withheld some evidence in order to present it in person. He was amazed when the adjudication appeared before he could do so. The Press Council replied that its leaflet 109 ('Guidance on Procedure for Complainants' – fifth edition 1978, sixth edition 1980) did not promise an oral hearing.[39] These leaflets were somewhat ambiguous, and could well have left a complainant with the impression that an oral hearing would normally follow.

It may be of some consolation to Frank Field that the most recent (seventh) edition of this leaflet makes clear, perhaps as a result of his representation, that only the newspaper editor or the council can insist upon an oral hearing. Nonetheless, clearing up the ambiguity does not meet Mr Field's criticism, which was supported by successful complainants such as Tony Smythe and Arthur Scargill, that the right to an oral hearing *is* of great importance. As a matter of ordinary fairness, complainants should be given the same right as editors to insist upon an oral hearing, although the council would of course be entitled to impose a reasonable limitation on the length.

The unfairness of the present position is emphasized by the fact that the council goes out of its way to encourage editors and journalists to insist upon the right to an oral hearing. In 1979 it issued a special memorandum to editors urging them to remind any journalists whose work is subject to complaint that 'if he wishes to appear in person in order to supplement his statement or to put his point of view, the Complaints Committee will hear him'.[40] This is not the only privilege available to the newspaper side: often national papers sidestep the ban on legal representation by having their defence to the complaint presented by a legally trained employee or legal manager. The complainant, on the other hand, is simply told 'There is no legal representation.'

Another feature of complaints committee hearings which surprised several respondents was that, when they attended for a second hearing, there were substantial changes in the composition of the committee. They felt, as one put it, 'as though our jury had changed in mid-trial'. Both Sappho and the Federation of Claimants' Unions criticized the social class composition of the committee which heard their complaints, and the lack of understanding displayed towards minority groups. Their criticisms, while valid enough at the time, have been met to some extent by recent appointments.

There is also ground for concern at the unfairness suffered by J.K. Purves, director of education for Dumfries and Galloway Regional Council. Mr Purves made a complaint to the Press Council about the failure of his local paper adequately to correct factual inaccuracies in an editorial which criticized him, surprisingly enough, for giving an interview to the media. The complaints committee decided that his case did not warrant adjudication by the council, and so declined to consider the merits of his complaint.[41] In consequence, no reasoned adjudication setting out the case for both sides and deciding where the merits lay, was ever made. When the local paper was informed, it published a story headed '*Standard* cleared by Press Council', and proceeded to give its own account of the facts. When the Press Council declines to adjudicate a complaint, it should *either* announce that in doing so it makes no finding on the issue in dispute *or,* if it does make such a finding, spell out with some care the reason why the complaint was so unjustified as not to merit an adjudication.

Form of adjudication Several complainants, both successful and unsuccessful, claimed that errors of fact crept into the adjudication, and maintained that they were given no opportunity to correct them prior to publication. The council, on the other hand, maintains that such an opportunity is always given. As a matter of course, the council sends to both parties by recorded delivery a copy of its adjudication approximately a week before its embargoed press-release date. This is accompanied merely by a form letter which reads:

> The Press Council has completed its inquiry into the complaint presented by you against [the newspaper]. I enclose for your information a document which sets out a draft narrative of the case together with the Adjudication which the Council proposes to issue for publication on the date stated. Please regard this statement as confidential until the time indicated.

There is no indication in this letter that the complainant is being given an opportunity to seek any amendment in the narrative of fact. The opportunity happens to exist, but the complainant is not told, much less invited to take any advantage of it. The dissatisfaction of those who complained of having no opportunity to correct inaccuracies can be appreciated, especially since there have been a number of cases where newspapers have pointed out factual errors which the council has rectified prior to the release of the adjudication.

Press Council in Action

The comments on the council's complaints procedure set out in this chapter arose from experiences of it between 1977 and 1981. Except where otherwise indicated, enquiry suggests they remain valid. It is instructive to compare them with evidence of the early stages of one of the council's most recent, and most important, complaints. It concerns allegations of fabrication of news – a breach of the most fundamental press ethic – by Britain's largest daily newspaper.

On 22 October 1982, the *Daily Mirror* published, editorially, a claim that the *Sun* was publishing deliberate lies. The *Sun* had carried what purported to be an interview with the widow of a Falklands soldier on the day after he had been posthumously awarded the Victoria Cross. It attributed a number of statements to the woman, Mrs McKay, which she was said to have made whilst 'hugging her children at their home in Rotherham, Yorkshire'. In fact, the *Mirror* alleged, Mrs McKay was in London at the time and had not spoken to the *Sun*. The 'quotes' were manufactured in the offices of the newspaper, with the help of secretaries who were asked how they would feel if *their* husbands had died winning the VC. The *Mirror*'s allegations were said to have derived from journalists working on the *Sun*. It alleged two other examples of similar fabrications of news by the *Sun*.

A Press Council genuinely concerned to maintain the highest professional standards in the British press could hardly ignore these serious and apparently substantiated allegations. It seems to have done so until, a fortnight later, a woman from Walthamstow wrote to the council summarizing the *Daily Mirror* article and pointing out the serious ethical issue it raised about the behaviour of the *Sun*. 'I would be grateful if you would regard this as a formal complaint and take the appropriate action,' the letter concluded.

The assistant director of the council, Charles White, replied on 8 November.

> Thank you for your letter of 3 Nov 82, which is not being treated at this stage as a formal complaint but as an inquiry . . . .
>
> It is not clear from your letter whether you wish to complain against the *Sun*, the *Daily Mirror*, or both. Could you clarify this?
>
> I would also ask you to bear in mind that a complaints committee would be no better placed than yourself to assess the truth of two conflicting newspaper stories unless it is provided with independent evidence supporting one version. If you wish to pursue a complaint, would you be able to provide such information for the complaints committee?

The original letter was expressed as a formal complaint. The council unhelpfully treated it as an enquiry, to be parried with a request for clarification of the obvious. The council, with all its claims to respect and obedience in Fleet Street, indicated that it is no better placed than an ordinary member of the public when it comes to discovering what goes on in newspaper offices. 'Unless your resources stretch to collecting independent evidence to challenge the word of News International, you might as well give up,' is the interpretation that some members of the public would put on that final paragraph.

The woman from Walthamstow was made of sterner stuff. She responded immediately, repeating that she wished to make a formal complaint, and patiently 'clarifying' the fact that this complaint was against the *Sun*. As for the council's professed inability 'to assess the truth of two conflicting newspaper stories', she gently pointed out that 'all you have to do, surely, is ask Mrs McKay whether she gave an interview to the *Sun* and whether the quotes ascribed to her in the paper were indeed made by her'.

The assistant director replied on 12 November. It was 'necessary' to clarify the position because 'you did not say precisely which newspaper you wished to make a complaint against'. The procedural formalities which had delayed the complaint were now in order, and it could proceed. The assistant director also said:

> I must also explain that it would be most inappropriate for the Press Council to make a complainant's case before adjudicating upon it. As I explained previously, it is the accuser's job to prove a case. The Council's job is to decide whether this has been done.
>
> Your letters will be treated as a complaint against the *Sun* and the correspondence will accordingly be forwarded to the editor. He may take this opportunity to get in touch with you direct.
>
> If he does not contact you within a reasonable time – say a fortnight – or if you are dissatisfied with his response and believe the matter warrants an investigation by the Council, you should write to the director again, enclosing copies of all letters you have written to or received from the newspaper and of any additional material you think may be helpful, including the *Daily Mirror* story of 22 Oct 82 and the stories published in the *Sun*.
>
> Your complaint will then be investigated with a view to submitting it to the Complaints Committee of the Council for consideration.

There are three things to be observed about the council's *modus operandi*:

(i) The council is not really accepting the complaint at this stage. It is merely passing it on, by post, to the editor in question. He may sort it out with the complainant, or the complainant may give up. In either case, the fact that there may have been a grave breach of ethical standards will not concern the council at all.

(ii) The onus is on the complainant to bring the matter back to the council, and to supply full documentation. The council is unwilling even to obtain for itself copies of the newspaper articles concerned, despite the seriousness of the allegation and the fact that they were published only a few weeks previously.

(iii) Should the complainant raise her head again, it will be as an 'accuser' with 'the job to prove a case'. The council will sit back and decide whether she has done her job as well as the legal manager of the *Sun* has done his job. The council's approach, in other than very exceptional cases like Thorpe and Sutcliffe, is not to 'investigate' at all. This word, which always figures in the council's description of its procedures, gives an incorrect impression. The council may arbitrate, but in the vast majority of cases it deems investigation 'inappropriate'. It will not pick up a telephone and ask Mrs McKay whether she really was interviewed by the *Sun*.

This simple detective exercise was soon performed by the 'Pendennis' column of the *Observer*. It reported that Mrs McKay's evidence on the point was emphatic. She said: 'I never spoke to the *Sun*. I know that; they know that. You can imagine what I think of the paper.' Meanwhile, the woman from Walthamstow was biding her 'reasonable time' in expectation of a response from the editor of the *Sun*. It did not come. So, after waiting for three weeks, she wrote again to the Press Council on 2 December, enclosing the newspaper back issues it had requested and the fresh evidence published in the *Observer*. A few weeks later the council replied that the evidence from the *Observer* was of no help – it was only 'hearsay' – that is, a statement which a possibly unreliable third party claimed to have heard Mrs McKay make. The Press Council was still not inclined to take any steps to hear for itself whether Mrs McKay would repeat the statement.

At the time of writing, this complaint is still under what the council chooses to call its investigation. The fact that it has been asked to give a ruling has now been reported in the national press, which may make the future course of this complaint somewhat atypical. The treatment of the complainant in the early stages, however, underlines the validity of many of the criticisms of the complaints procedure made by those who experienced it in 1977–81.

Conclusions

● There is a high level of dissatisfaction among those members of the public who accept the Press Council's invitation to complain against newspapers.

● The council does not, despite its public statements to the contrary, offer prompt or speedy redress for inaccuracy or breaches of ethical standards by the press.

● The delay which regularly attends the council's deliberations operates to destroy the purpose of many complaints, so that its service is frequently ineffective. This delay is not apparent when the adjudication is published, because the council omits from the text all reference to the date when the complaint was lodged. A former member of the council, Charles Wintour, wrote in 1982: 'Adjudications issued by the council *cunningly omit* the date of the original story.' Others may find a different adverb to describe the council's policy in this respect. It seems clearly desirable that every adjudication should carry both the date of the original article and the date on which the complaint was first received.

● In cases of distortion and inaccuracy, the Press Council is not a satisfactory alternative to legal action. Victims who are wealthy enough to retain lawyers often find that newspapers publish immediate and prominent retractions and apologies, and sometimes pay damages, under threat of a suit for libel. By comparison, the Press Council adjudication procedure takes many months, and has no power to direct a prominent correction, an apology, or damages. In a society which does not make legal aid available for libel actions, the Press Council offers a 'poor person's libel service' which may be a poor second-best to the legal weapon available to the wealthy.

● In some cases of inordinate delay complainants are partly at fault. However, the prime responsibility for debilitating delays rests with the Press Council, and is occasioned by its own internal procedures. The following are among the main causes:

(i) The Press Council makes a practice of automatically referring every complaint to the newspaper editor in question, and refuses to accept the complaint until he or she has finally responded to the complainant. In many cases, the complainant

only approaches the Press Council after the editor has refused satisfaction: in such cases, the council's policy (which can be responsible for several weeks' initial delay) is pointless.

(ii) The Press Council's officers are strangely reluctant to make use of the telephone. In some cases an astonishing number of letters passes back and forth, after the initial complaint, about minor linguistic details of complaint formulation and requests for submission of further evidence. Most of these matters could be expeditiously dealt with by telephone calls on the day the complaint is received.

(iii) In a few cases, some delay is inevitable to ascertain disputed facts. But the point of many complaints – certainly those alleging breaches of ethics – can be appreciated from a glance at the newspaper item concerned. In the case of Blaine Stothard and the *Daily Mail*, described in the next chapter, there was a ten-month delay in deciding whether a cartoon without a caption was in breach of a professional standard.

(iv) The full Press Council has to approve every adjudication, and it normally meets only once every two months. This is a potent reason for delay, and is a weakness inherent in the way the Press Council is run. The council could meet more often, or adjudications could be agreed between members by post or telephone, or the responsibility of approving them could be delegated to a representative committee of the council. Charles Wintour sensibly suggests that 'the council should elect an emergency team of five to deal with the really urgent cases'.

● Certain conclusions can be drawn about the social class and the level of education and worldly wisdom of successful complainants. Success predominantly attends those from the upper and middle classes, with attainments in education, professional skill and/or articulateness. It is rare to find a successful 'working-class' complainant. When complaints are made on behalf of such persons by MPs or organizations such as MIND or Shelter, however, they stand a reasonable prospect of success.

● The Press Council's adoption of an adversarial procedure, as distinct from an inquisitory one, places a high premium on the complainant's skill in written and sometimes oral argument. The council makes frequent reference to its 'investigations', but this is an exaggeration: it has no investigators, and its enquiries consist of asking the parties for written accounts and evidence which make up a dossier to be considered by the complaints committee. Unless the council is prepared to undertake an investigative role, and to take the initiative on apparently justifiable complaints, it will continue to provide redress only for those who are both determined and articulate.

● The legal waiver, which is itself an indication of the council's claim to offer an alternative to legal redress, is resented by complainants. There are comparatively few instances where recourse to a waiver is really justified.

● There is an enormous number of 'withdrawn' complaints. It is likely that some of these complaints are withdrawn because of the obstacles which become apparent to complainants after initial contact with the council. The delay, the difficulty of formulating a complaint about breach of a 'standard' where no yardstick exists, and the legal waiver must all contribute to a complainant's sense that he or she is about to tread through a procedural minefield, as an 'accuser' who bears a heavy burden of proof.

● The right of the newspaper but not of the complainant to demand an oral hearing gives the press an unfair advantage.

● Lawyers frequently appear at the council's oral hearings, representing the newspaper which employs them. This is apt to give an unfair advantage to the press. Complainants should be allowed to have their case presented by a friend or representative, whether a lawyer or otherwise. One consequence might be that the complaint is presented more effectively and expeditiously.

● The council should specifically invite the parties to correct any factual errors in its adjudications before they are issued to the press.

● The council should pay the reasonable expenses of all successful complainants. This should not only include travelling expenses (which are now paid when requested) but photocopying, the cost of collecting witness statements, and so forth.

● The council needs a full-time chairman and an expanded staff if it is to begin to monitor and investigate press conduct, bring its annual reports out in reasonable time, and deal expeditiously with complaints.

● The problems relating to publication of complaints are endemic in the council's present structure. Some method must be found to ensure that:

(i) offending journals publish the adjudication, and do so in full and without misleading headings;

(ii) publication is of sufficient prominence to redress the original imbalance;

(iii) publication, although in a more summary form, is provided by all papers which pick up the offending story, even though their conduct has not been in issue before the council.

● There is a need to implement a number of the recommendations made by the third Royal Commission, including the following:

(i) The council should be supplied with more staff and money to advertise its services. If the money is not forthcoming, there is no reason why national and local newspapers could not agree to publish, perhaps once every three months, a free advertisement explaining the purposes and procedures of the Press Council.

(ii) The council should obtain undertakings from newspapers that they will publish complaints upheld against them on their front page. Implementation of this recommendation would satisfactorily resolve the problem of 'prominence'. In the case of a long adjudication, it would be sufficient if the gist of the ruling appeared as front-page news, and the elaboration of facts and arguments was carried over to a subsequent page.

(iii) The council should initiate more complaints itself, and monitor and publicize the record of persistent offenders.

This chapter has reflected the vantage point of members of the public, because it is they who are charged by the council with the burden of locating, investigating, and finally proving the cases in which press conduct falls short of acceptable standards. There is another side to the story, and it is told by the majority of editors and journalists who take the complaint and the council seriously enough to mount a thorough defence. A great deal of investigation and paperwork goes on, inside newspaper offices, to prepare responses and to reply to council requests. From the press point of view, there is also a frustration at the council's delays, and at its inability to make simple enquiries which would abort unjustified complaints at an early stage. Editors point with some force to trivial complaints which have run the gamut of the council's procedures before being dismissed, and they are understandably annoyed at the standards set by some adjudications, which appear unduly solicitous of powerful people (the most common examples being Royalty and trade-union general secretaries). Inevitably, where value-judgements are involved, there will be legitimate differences of opinion between the press and the Press Councillors. The message of this chapter is not that the council's procedures favour the press, but that they favour unnecessary delay, undue formality and unsatisfactory redress. Both complainants and the newspapers complained against would, in the long run, benefit from thorough-going reforms.

4
Professional Standards

In 1973, some editors told the Younger Committee on Privacy that the Press Council was 'respected, feared and obeyed'.[1] The council repeatedly publishes this tribute, because these qualities are essential for it to uphold the second article of its constitution, namely its obligation 'To maintain the character of the British Press in accordance with the highest professional and commercial standards'. This chapter examines the level of obedience that the council is able to command, a decade after the Younger Committee, for its rulings on professional standards. Although it is not clear what the constitution means by commercial standards, it will become apparent that commercial pressures have encouraged some newspapers to sacrifice high standards in the interests of higher circulation.

Any discussion of journalistic ethics must allow that the prime purpose of the press – of proprietors, editors and journalists – is, in the words of the third Royal Commission, 'to advance the public interest by publishing the facts and opinions without which a democratic electorate cannot make responsible judgements'.[2] In fulfilling that task, journalists may have no alternative but to behave in devious and dishonest ways: to invade privacy, to wave cheque-books at criminal associates, and even to break the law. The *Sunday Times* obtained some of the material for its celebrated Thalidomide campaign by a blatant use of its cheque-book. In America, the unravelling of Watergate was achieved by a series of manoeuvres which offend 'the highest professional standards' unless it is accepted that the highest standard of all is to provide the public with accurate information on matters of genuine public interest.

Journalism is the exercise by occupation of the right to free expression available to every citizen. The right to write is therefore impossible to reconcile with proposals to license journalists, and to expel or suspend them from a professional register for breaches of ethics. But there is one important distinction to be made between freedom of expression and freedom of the press: the former is an aspect of individual liberty, the latter a prerogative exercised by an industry. What becomes of the individual's freedom to express a reply to a personal attack, for example, when the editor of a local newspaper monopoly exerts the freedom of the press to deny that individual any space to have the reply published? The distinction to be drawn is between the exercise of an individual right, and the exercise of editorial power which may or may not promote the public interest. It is in assessing the morality of particular exercises of editorial discretion that ethics and standards become relevant.

In Britain, editorial decisions may suffer three kinds of adverse consequences. They may entail punishment as a criminal (e.g. for contempt or breaches of official secrecy), they may provoke damages in a civil action (e.g. for libel or breach of copyright or confidence) or they may receive censure from the Press Council. There can be no doubt that the criminal and civil law bears too heavily on the press in its role as provider of information on matters of public interest, and the degree of unnecessary restraint is indicated in Chapter 5. But there is also no doubt that their consequences – the risk of prison, or of adverse awards of legal costs and damages, are powerful deterrents which inevitably affect the decision to publish. Press Council censure, on the other hand, can only deter if it causes serious, albeit retrospective, embarrassment.

The theory is that if a newspaper reports an adverse Press Council adjudication prominently and in sufficient detail for readers to appreciate the nature of its lapse from professional standards, and rival newspapers give the adjudication sufficient publicity, the principles stated in the judgement will remain in the consciousness of editors and journalists in the future. They will become part of press lore, if not press law. Nobody likes being criticized, the theory goes, and hence everybody will take care to avoid attracting similar criticism in future. In other words, the Press Council achieves acceptance of extra-legal standards by the psychological impact of the principles it lays down in the course of deciding particular complaints. It has no power, other than the force of its own words. That force can be felt only by proprietors, editors and journalists in the milieu in which they work and socialize. They are unlikely to feel it from any other quarter: readers will not stop buying a newspaper simply because it has suffered a series of adverse adjudications. If fear of the Press Council is not fear of losing liberty or money or circulation, it can only be fear of losing face.

The effectiveness of the Press Council thus depends heavily upon editorial reaction to its adjudications. Occasionally, editors refuse to publish these at all. But most adjudications are published in the newspaper to which they relate, although seldom with great prominence and often in truncated form. Those which have not involved a major investigation, like that into the Sutcliffe affair, are rarely attended by editorial soul-searching or examination of principles. They are published out of duty; the very fact that for the last decade there has been no independent published analysis of the ethical standards developed by the Press Council is an indication of its failure to make those standards a live issue. The absence of a code of conduct may be partly to blame: it is all too easy to dismiss particular adjudications as isolated instances which turn on their own facts. It is difficult to credit an organization with 'maintaining the highest professional standards' when it cannot describe in a coherent code the standards which it exists to maintain.

There are, however, exceptional cases where the censured editor has publicly reacted to the adjudication. Instead of inviting informed public debate, however, some of these reactions have called into question the value of the council, because they have taken the form of reprisals against both the council and its successful complainants. In these cases, the newspaper has used the adverse adjudication as a springboard, not only for an unabashed repetition of its offending article, but for heaping abuse on the complainant and the council. In place of respect and obedience, the council receives contempt and derision. The perils of making a successful complaint to the Press Council against a large-circulation national newspaper are demonstrated in the following examples.

The Daily Mail In May 1979 Blaine Stothard complained on behalf of fellow branch members of the National Union of Teachers against a cartoon published in the *Daily Mail* after the death of Blair Peach. Ten months later the council upheld the complaint, on the basis that the suggestion made by the cartoon, which it took to be that members of the Anti-Nazi League were out to kill policemen, was 'false and highly offensive'.[3] The day after the adjudication was published, the editor of the newspaper devoted two pages to a full-blooded attack upon both Mr Stothard and the Press Council, republishing the 'false and highly offensive' cartoon in the process. Mr Stothard's colleagues wrote a letter in defence of his position, which the editor refused to publish ('it is clear to me that you have not understood my article. Therefore, I see no point in further correspondence on this matter').[4] Mr Stothard, who had now suffered severe criticism for approaching the council with a complaint in the first place, wrote to it again informing it of the newspaper's reaction. 'Many thanks for keeping the Council informed' was the bland response from the assistant secretary. 'I can take no further action now that the adjudication has been published.'[5]

There may be legitimate doubts about the wisdom of this particular Press Council adjudication. But it is astonishing that the organization washed its hands of a case in which its own adjudication had been made the occasion for an attack upon the complainant. The editor's refusal to publish a letter in defence of the complaint raised the issue of the council's much vaunted 'right of reply'. Its own failure to reply to the editor's criticism of its adjudication meant that its case – which was also that of Mr Stothard – was lost by default.

The response of the assistant secretary to Blaine Stothard shows that the Press Council failed to protect its own credibility on the grounds that it could do nothing. Perhaps the assistant secretary meant that it could do nothing of very much consequence. Without contractual or statutory powers, it can issue rebuke after rebuke, and have each rebuke made the occasion for a devastating attack on itself and on its luckless complainant.

Labour MP Maureen Colquhoun complained that the *Daily Mail* had invaded the privacy of herself and a friend. The council deplored the newspaper's 'serious harassment' of the friend; the treatment of Maureen Colquhoun, however, was 'just over the border into what is permissible'.[6] The *Daily Mail,* assisted by the Press Council's last-minute agreement to water down the wording of the adjudication, reported it in such a biased way as to suggest that the council had approved of the newspaper's conduct. The Royal Commission felt the council was at fault in giving the newspaper the opportunity to claim the adjudication as a victory: 'This episode was bound to cast doubts on the impartiality of the Press Council and to damage its credibility as an independent body by displaying excessive regard for the susceptibilities of a newspaper which at no stage in the proceedings had behaved in a manner to warrant it. We hope that in future the Press Council will be more vigilant in demonstrating the independence and impartiality to which it lays claim.'[7]

The Sun A newspaper is perfectly free to exaggerate and to distort Press Council adjudications which condemn it for exaggeration and distortion. From this 'catch-22' there is no escape for a body which cannot enforce its judgements, or even ensure that they are published in full.

On 8 October 1982, the Press Council issued an adjudication relating to reports in the *Sun* in March 1981 (a delay of eighteen months). These reports were headed: 'Day the blacks ran riot in London'. They contained lurid accounts of how 'a frenzied mob took part in an orgy of looting and destruction in the West End . . . the rampage began as thousands of blacks stormed up Fleet Street'. A march of 5000 people protesting about the deaths of thirteen black children in a Deptford fire had undoubtedly attracted some fringe violence. But having considered all the evidence supplied to it, the council issued the following press release.[8]

THE *SUN*: SENSATIONAL REPORT CONDEMNED
Although a national newspaper report of the protest march following the Deptford fire disaster was not aimed at damaging racial harmony or systematically distorted, it was highly sensationalised, contained inaccuracies and gross exaggerations, and lacked sensitivity, the Press Council found today. The Council condemned the *Sun*'s 'exaggerated and sensational treatment of a difficult and sensitive matter'.

The full adjudication read:

The Press Council does not find that the *Sun* systematically distorted its report of this protest march or that the report was aimed by the newspaper at damaging racial harmony, but the report did contain inaccuracies, gross exaggerations and other grounds for serious criticism.

Most importantly, in the Press Council's view, it was a highly sensationalised account markedly lacking in sensitivity. The introduction to the report was so exaggerated as to be insupportable, but the Press Council regards the repeated play on the word 'black' in headlines as merely an unfortunate attempt at brightness rather than malicious or pejorative.

When Lord Scarman's report on the Brixton Riots was published the Press Council said it supported his call to editors to accept responsibility for assessing the likely impact on events of their reporting, and to ensure balance in the coverage of disorder, and his conclusion that editors and journalists should pay continuous attention to the social implications of their power to influence attitudes.

Such understanding was lacking in this case, and the Press Council condemns the report's exaggerated and sensational treatment of a difficult and sensitive matter. The picture it painted of a day of major violence was untrue, but there was certainly fringe violence and disorder which probably did more damage to good race relations than the *Sun*'s report did.

To the extent set out in this adjudication the complaints against the *Sun* were upheld.

In the *Sun* on 8 October, this adjudication was derided in a full column front-page editorial, under the proud banner headline 'PAPER THEY CAN'T GAG' (which was true enough). The editorial continued for a further full column on page two, which was headed 'THE TRUTH'. Unfortunately, however, it wasn't. The editorial said: 'The Council even takes us to task because in our headlines we used the word "black", and more than once, too. Let's dispose of this dreadful sin first.' The next three column inches of the editorial were devoted to disposing of the 'dreadful sin' for which the *Sun* claimed to have been 'taken to task'. On the contrary, the adjudication had specifically acquitted it of this complaint, on the ground that 'the repeated play on the word "black" in headlines' was 'merely an unfortunate attempt at brightness rather than malicious or pejorative'. This passage was not reported, either in the editorial or in the news report on a subsequent full page. The newspaper would have had at least five days to study the 300-word adjudication, yet it chose to give its readers the impression that the Press Council had upheld the one complaint against its report that the council had gone out of its way to excuse.

In the same vein, the editorial went on to quote a passage from the *Sun*'s original editorial published on the day after the demonstration. It had written of 'A day in which the cause of inter-racial harmony was seriously damaged by a few black hotheads'. Now, it asked its readers, 'was that a wilful malicious distortion? Was that unfair to black people?' No, it was not, and the Press Council's adjudication does not suggest that it was. On the contrary, the council stated: 'There was certainly fringe violence and disorder which probably did more damage to race relations than the *Sun*'s report did.' The Press Council censured the *Sun* for publishing reports which painted a false picture of 'a day of major violence', and not for condemning 'a few hotheads'. The editorial concluded, in heavy type, '**We shall go on reporting the truth. The whole truth.**'

The *Sun* devoted a later page to a 'report' of the adjudication, under the banner: 'NO 1 PAPER RAPPED – FOR TELLING THE TRUTH'. It did not set out the whole adjudication, but it did take the opportunity to repeat some of its original pictures and stories, under the heading: 'Bloody trail of the Demo Hordes'.

The Press Council may believe that it is still 'respected, feared, and obeyed' in Fleet Street. The response to its adjudication by the *Sun* puts that claim in perspective, and shows that the Press Council itself cannot on occasion obtain a fair hearing from Fleet Street. In this adjudication the council had gone out of its way to be fair to the newspaper. It took eighteen months to reach its decision, a delay which it explained in part as being caused by a problem 'in resolving with the newspaper a potential danger that some of the journalists concerned might be placed in double jeopardy' (it did not make clear how this double jeopardy might arise: the Press Council puts no journalist in single jeopardy). It listened to evidence called by the *Sun*. It was addressed at length by Henry Douglas, a long-time member of the council and the newspaper's legal manager (complainants, it will be recalled, are not allowed legal representation). The adjudication was scrupulous to acquit the newspaper and its journalists of systematic distortion or any desire to damage racial harmony. Yet, at the end of the day, its adjudication was used as a pretext for editorial self-congratulation: 'The *Sun* is flattered to be singled out as the target for complaint.' When the largest circulation daily in Fleet Street wears its condemnation with pride, what is left of 'respect, fear and obedience'?

A Press Council which cannot protect itself from distortion and inaccuracies is unlikely to be able to provide adequate protection for complainants. No less than thirty-three individuals and organizations complained about the *Sun*'s coverage of the Deptford march. All but six of them fell by the familiar wayside in the eighteen-month journey towards adjudication. Those who persisted included teachers at Goldsmiths College, several charities, and the Lewisham Council for Community Relations. They were described in the *Sun*'s editorial as 'a weird rag-bag of pressure groups and social pleaders' who had waged 'a squalid campaign' and presented 'claptrap' as evidence. Complainants cannot expect to be shielded from fair comment, but to describe their campaign as 'squalid' and their evidence as 'claptrap' (without setting out their evidence to allow readers to judge for themselves) is in no sense fair.

It is illuminating to compare the way the *Sun* treated the Deptford complainants with the extraordinary precautions its stablemate, the *News of the World,* took in the same year to shield its own journalists from possible Press Council criticism. That newspaper published an interview with an 'ex-mistress' who had given evidence at the trial for murder of Dr Paul Vickers. The woman complained to the council that the quotations attributed to her were bogus. The newspaper, through its legal manager Henry Douglas, told the council that it would refuse to publish any adjudication which might imply that its reporter had 'fabricated' any part of her story. Since this was the nub of the complaint, the newspaper's attitude amounted both to a pre-judgement and a threat. Had the complaints committee been a real court the newspaper would have been guilty of a serious contempt. But the Press Council, when it published its adjudication in August 1982, could only 'deplore' this refusal to accept a 'moral obligation' to publish whatever the result.[9] It felt it necessary to explain that its decision (which in fact exonerated the reporter) was uninfluenced by the newspaper's stated determination to censor an unfavourable judgement.

The implications of these two recent cases are disturbing for anyone wishing to complain against the *Sun* or the *News of the World.* They 'submitted' to Press Council adjudications. But in one case, they indicated before the adjudication was reached that they would not publish it if it went against them. In the other, which did go against them, they published a distorted interpretation as an excuse for condemning the Press Council and humiliating those who were held to have justly complained. What advice can now be given to any person who contemplates taking these papers to the Press Council: 'heads they win, and tails you lose'? After the Deptford demonstration adjudication, the Press Council was silent. In the Vickers adjudication, it lamented the newspaper's threat to disobey a 'moral obligation'. Some 'moral obligations' are obviously not worth the paper they may not be printed in.

The Quality of Press Council Adjudication

Press Council adjudications are necessarily short, so as to provide a reasonable incentive for newspapers to carry most if not all of the adjudication in a news report. The full flavour of cases cannot be appreciated without resort to the factual background, which summarizes the contentions of both parties, and which is published in full only in the *UK Press Gazette*. These factual backgrounds, however, are simply reports of the arguments, and do not contain any elaboration by the council of the principles involved in its decision. In consequence, its individual adjudications do not contain support, by way of argument or statement of precedent, for the principle (if any) on which the case turns. This is only provided on the rare occasions when the council mounts a major enquiry or issues a Declaration of Principle. The main Declarations concern cheque-book journalism (1966, amended 1983), the right of the press to be partisan (1967), and privacy (1976). Other standards could be developed into Declarations of Principle, which could in turn be embodied in the code of conduct which the council has for so long resisted. This would answer the criticism of adjudications made by Alexander Irvine QC, as part of a private study which was submitted to the third Royal Commission. 'Press Council decisions,' he concluded, 'are reported too shortly, do not appear to be fully or clearly reasoned and in sum often lack any intellectual coherence or consistency of policy.'[10]

The complaints committees of the council strive to reach a result which is fair to both sides. They are reluctant to condemn without extenuation, or to dismiss without credit. The bias towards the press which was once apparent has in part been corrected. There are some recent adjudications which may appear unduly favourable to the newspapers, but there are others, particularly involving questions of taste, which seem unduly censorious. There is, however, little evidence to support the assertion that the council's work has contributed greatly towards maintaining high professional standards. Some obvious grounds for censure – failure to afford a right of reply, and unjustifiable invasion of privacy – have been condemned by the council from its outset. Yet still they occur and are censured time and again. The third Royal Commission found 'flagrant breaches of acceptable standards' and 'inexcusable intrusions into privacy'.[11] The instances it mentions (intrusion into the lives of children and relatives of famous persons; harassment of bereaved parents) seem to occur as regularly as ever, despite repeated Press Council censure.

There are two main reasons for disobeying council edicts: they lack any measure of enforcement which might deter circulation-seeking editors, and in some cases at least they are lacking in coherent and acceptable definition. These two weaknesses can be observed in council rulings in three important areas: cheque-book journalism, the right of reply, and privacy.

Declaration on Payments to Witnesses, Criminals and Associates

Payments to witnesses After the chief prosecution witness in the Moors murder trial in 1966 stated that he was in weekly receipt of payments from a newspaper, the council issued its first Declaration of Principle: 'No payment or offer of payment should be made by a newspaper to any person known or reasonably expected to be a witness in criminal proceedings already begun . . . until they have been concluded.' The public policy considerations behind this rule are manifest. Justice must be done on the basis of evidence sworn and tested in the courtroom. The objection to press deals with prospective witnesses is that bought witnesses become sold on their stories. They are tempted to exaggerate evidence in order to increase its saleability, and they may become committed to inaccurate stories ghosted by reporters and have a financial inducement to stick to them in the witness box. There are generally thought to be two ways in which society may guard against this danger of polluted justice: by the Press Council enforcing its Declaration of Principle, or by making the conduct a criminal offence. In this respect, Press Council authority is a clear alternative to legal regulation.

The council has failed to make its Declaration bite. In 1978 it was flagrantly breached by the *Sunday Telegraph,* which concluded a pre-trial contract with Peter Bessell, chief prosecution witness in the trial of Jeremy Thorpe and others on charges of conspiracy to murder. The newspaper paid Bessell £25,000 down, with an 'escalation clause' in the contract which provided a further £25,000 in the event (which could only have come about if Bessell's evidence were believed) of Thorpe being convicted. This deal destroyed Bessell's credibility at the trial. After a long enquiry, the Press Council passed 'the severest censure' on the newspaper for 'reckless disregard of the predictable consequences'. It announced that this censure would deter future breaches of the Declaration, and concluded its seventy-five-page report with the simple but unargued assertion: 'The Council would be opposed to any legislation in this field.'[12]

A little over one year later, Peter Sutcliffe was arrested and charged with thirteen murders. In immediate and blatant defiance of the Declaration, a number of national newspapers made large cash offers to persons who were, at that stage, certain to be called to give evidence in the event of a contested trial. At least three major newspapers – the *Daily Mail,* the *Observer* and the *News of the World* – were involved within a few weeks of the arrest in suggesting deals to the Sutcliffes' solicitors whereby six-figure sums would accrue to Mrs Sutcliffe. When certain of these manoeuvres leaked out – in *Private Eye,* not in national newspapers – the public outrage which erupted was unparalleled in the history of Fleet Street. It is true to say that the indignation was largely prompted by the spectre of enormous sums of money being paid to a person because she was the wife of an alleged mass-murderer. But at Sutcliffe's eventual trial, judicial displeasure was also expressed when several witnesses owned up to cash deals with particular newspapers. One witness had become, in effect, the property of the *Sunday People,* which was paying him £80 a week and harbouring him so securely that even the police were not allowed to contact him except through the offices of the newspaper. The Press Council responded to the public concern by announcing a full enquiry. Its report, 'Press Conduct in the Sutcliffe Case', took two years to produce. When it was published, in February 1983, the council condemned a number of newspapers for making payments to persons who could reasonably have been expected to testify. It did not consider, however, that its Declaration of Principle, prohibiting pre-trial payments to potential witnesses, needed amendment or extension, much less statutory force.[13]

The Press Council's blanket rule against offers of payment to potential witnesses in criminal cases occasions severe practical difficulties for newspaper editors. It is simply impossible to foretell, in the days after arrest, how the prosecution and defence cases are likely to be developed. In addition, the Declaration makes no distinction between a witness to disputed facts (whose testimony must be kept free from any influence) and a witness to matters of formal record, whose evidence may well merely be read to the court. Friends and family members are always potential defence witnesses, but usually only to the character of the defendant or to matters which would be urged in mitigation after a conviction or plea of guilty has been recorded. The interests of justice which are served by a rule against paying witnesses do not apply with very great force to witnesses whose evidence is unlikely to affect the central issue of guilt or innocence. That said, however, there can be no justification for those newspapers which, within a few days of Sutcliffe's arrest, paid a large cash sum to the prostitute in the car with him at the time (potentially a crucial witness of fact) and offered enormous sums to Mrs Sutcliffe (potentially a vital alibi witness). The newspapers concerned defended their actions on the ground that police had informed them that Sutcliffe had confessed, but experienced editors must be aware that defendants frequently repudiate confessions made in police custody.

There is no doubt that the Press Council Declaration on witness payments will continue to be broken. Only a week before the Sutcliffe report appeared, the *Daily Mail* bought exclusive rights to the story of Sue Stephens, who had been a passenger in the car in which Stephen Waldorf was shot by police in mistake for a wanted man. Clearly she would be a vital witness in charges brought against police officers for the attempted murder of Waldorf. When sensational cases of this sort arise, newspapers simply will not bow to the council's moral persuasion.

But the alternative – giving the Declaration legal force – also has drawbacks. There will remain areas of uncertainty, as the question of who will give evidence depends on contingencies in the development of prosecution and defence cases. The council's existing Declaration is unqualified by any consideration of public interest. Yet the Thalidomide campaign was based on material supplied to the *Sunday Times* by an expert witness who was paid £5000 for it, before the civil litigation over the drug had come to trial. [14] In 1976, serious charges against thirty-one people were dropped after David May of the *Sunday Times* found and interviewed a vital witness. The witness, feeling himself protected by that newspaper's prestige at the time, made allegations of police corruption which he had been afraid to reveal to the authorities. [15] Had he required a payment – to remove himself, for example, from an area where he might well suffer police reprisals – there would have been a strong public-interest argument for accommodating him. A statutory ban on payments to potential witnesses, therefore, while it would eradicate the danger of purchased perjury, would equally work against the occasional public-interest revelation.

There can be no doubt that contingency payments of the sort

offered to Peter Bessell present a serious threat to the administration of justice. The additional reward for obtaining a conviction is an incentive to exaggerate the evidence for the prosecution: if the contingency payment is revealed, the prosecution is likely to miscarry because the credibility of the witness is destroyed. Such payments should be outlawed, not by Press Council declarations, but by the law of the land. The law of contempt, which punishes actions which carry a substantial risk of serious prejudice to court proceedings, is probably sufficiently broad to encompass contingency payments, and it is unfortunate that the Attorney General did not confirm the position by prosecuting the *Sunday Telegraph* over its contract with Bessell. A wider blanket ban on any payment to a potential witness would be undesirable. A reasonable balance between the demands of justice and the need to permit newspapers to seek public-interest stories might be achieved by a law which obliged newspapers which interviewed potential witnesses in criminal cases to notify both prosecution and defence of the fact, and of the substance of any statement or material evidence obtained as a result. In the David May case described above, the newspaper immediately supplied a transcript of the interview to both sides; the trial, which was already in progress, collapsed when (as a result of the newspaper's action) the witness was subpoenaed and repeated his allegations under oath. It would have been outrageous had the newspaper held back its information until the defendants had been convicted and sentenced. An obligation on newspaper editors to disclose their dealings with potential witnesses would allow the court to evaluate that evidence in the light of such influence as the payment may have exerted: it would also work as a deterrent against making deals which could not retrospectively be justified on public-interest grounds.

Payments to criminals and associates The 1966 Declaration of Principle goes on to provide that 'No payment should be made for feature articles to persons engaged in crime or other notorious behaviour where the public interest does not warrant it.' Newspapers, of course, usually judge that the public interest *does* warrant it, and often they are right. The Press Council verdicts are inconsistent. A newspaper was censured for publishing articles by the wife of train robber Charles Wilson, although at different times articles by the wives of two other train robbers were held to be justifiable. The Press Council took the highly unusual course of initiating its own complaint in order to censure the publication of Christine Keeler's memoirs in 1969, although it took no action some years later in respect of the more lurid recollections of Mandy Rice-Davies. In 1967 the *Sun* was strongly censured for paying to publish the memoirs of Ronald Biggs; in 1981 it was censured for 'inexcusably repeating' that very offence in a 'flagrant violation' of the Declaration of Principle. This is perhaps an example of consistency at the expense of common sense: Biggs had not been 'engaged in crime' for many years, and his account of an attempt to kidnap and to extradite him was not without some public interest.

In 1983 the council tightened up its Declaration in response to the behaviour of the press in offering enormous sums of money to Mrs Sonia Sutcliffe, for no reason other than that she was the wife of a notorious mass-murderer. The 'blood money' amounted variously to £80,000 (*Daily Express*); £100,000 (*Observer*); and £110,000 (*News of the World*). The *Daily Mail* spoke of sums in excess of five figures, the *Daily Mirror* promised to exceed any rival offer, and the *Yorkshire Post* hazarded £1 million as the amount it could obtain for her by syndicating an exclusive story on the day her husband's trial ended. Reacting to this immoral auction, the council announced two amendments to its Declaration.[16]

(i) A ban, not only on direct or indirect payments to criminals, but also to their associates, including family, friends, neighbours and colleagues.

(ii) The 'public interest' justification would not apply, save in very exceptional cases.

Those newspapers which reacted editorially to the amended Declaration pointed out that it simply would not work in the harsh realities of the market-place. Some newspapers were cautiously critical, others openly defiant. The consensus of Fleet Street was best summed up by Michael Leapman in the *Daily Express*:

> The Press certainly will not – and should not – let itself be deflected from its function of telling people as much as it can about issues that interest them, however distasteful. Sometimes such information will have to be bought from people that editors, in a perfect world, would prefer not to do business with. A newspaper's principal obligation is to give its readers the fullest possible story.[17]

There can be no doubt that the council's 1983 Declaration on 'blood money' will not be honoured by newspaper editors. It is, indeed, the first of its edicts which a substantial number of editors have publicly repudiated, rather than privately ignored. If the payment of 'blood money' is to be stopped, it must be done by specific legislation.

But once again, legislation to outlaw cheque-book journalism of this sort would come up against insuperable difficulties of definition, of the sort which the council has already encountered over the Biggs and Keeler memoirs. Could 'blood money' be paid by a newspaper for serialization rights of a book about Watergate by Richard Nixon (an 'unindicted co-conspirator', as well as a 'friend, neighbour and colleague' of the men who were convicted), or a book about the war by Albert Speer (a war criminal), or a book about political conspiracy trials by Peter Hain (who was once convicted of a political conspiracy to trespass on cricket pitches)? It is likely that the end result of a law against press payments to criminals and their associates would be to deter criminals from revealing their associations with powerful people. In such cases, shady characters with public-interest stories to tell are often in genuine need of some remuneration for telling them. If they are prepared to go public with revelations about policemen or employers or persons in authority, they need financial protection against reprisals. The question, always, is whether the importance of the story and the exigencies of its author justify the size of the payment. That question must be answered by editors, in the first place. But should their answers not be heard, loudly and clearly, by the public as well?

The most important aspect of the Press Council's enquiry into 'Press Conduct in the Sutcliffe Case' was that in its course the council discovered, to its chagrin, that editors and executives of certain national newspapers were prepared to mislead it about their plans to pay witnesses and members of the Sutcliffe family. The editor of the *Daily Express* gave misleading answers to the council's questions, and was subject to 'astonishing' lapses of memory.[18] The *News of the World* displayed a 'lack of candour' by refusing to disclose relevant material;[19] the editor of the *Yorkshire Post* attempted to mislead the council;[20] and the *Daily Mail* deliberately hampered the council's enquiry by withholding vital evidence.[21] These attempts to suppress the truth were only revealed when Sutcliffe's solicitor handed over his correspondence file. Editors prepared to mislead the Press Council may have much less hesitation in misleading their own readers.

This is where the law must take a stand. The best working test of whether an exercise in cheque-book journalism is justified is whether or not the newspaper is prepared to own up to it. Whenever a newspaper publishes a story bought for more than a nominal sum from a criminal or associate, there should be a legal obligation to carry alongside it, in heavy type, a full statement of the amount of the payment. Such a law would not infringe press freedom: on the contrary, it would ensure the disclosure of information of genuine public interest. Readers would be alerted to the dangers of fabrication and exaggeration, by being put in a position to judge whether the sensations in the story might be related to the sensation its author felt when receiving a large cash sum for telling it. The obligation to disclose would positively deter editors from making payments which could not be openly justified.

One aspect of cheque-book journalism which could be ended by a simple amendment to the Copyright Act involves the purchase by newspapers or news agencies of an exclusive right to exploit family snap-shots of notorious criminals. If relatives are paid large sums by a particular news group for the exclusive copyright in a photograph, the law will prevent rival papers from publishing the same picture, however much a matter of public interest it has become, without the permission of the copyright holder. This market in the memorabilia of mass murder and the like would collapse overnight if the law were changed to permit all media to publish such photogaphs for the purpose of reporting current events. Section 6 of the Copyright Act 1956 allows extracts from copyrightable literary works to be published for this purpose, provided there is a proper acknowledgement. The addition of the word 'photographs' in the Section would accomplish the desired reform. News should not be the subject of copyright, and photographs which are specially newsworthy should not be confined to one newspaper merely because it happened to be the highest bidder.

In sum, the council's Declaration on payments to witnesses, criminals and associates is a counsel of perfection which editors will continue to ignore when it suits them, sometimes in the pursuit of revelations of genuine public interest, but more often in order to provide sensational stories of prurient rather than public interest. It would not be in the public interest to give statutory force to the Declaration, although certain changes in the law are required to safeguard the trial process against the danger of evidence being exaggerated or discredited by media payments. The crime of contempt should extend to cover contingency deals of the kind made between the *Sunday Telegraph* and Peter Bessell before the Thorpe trial. Newspapers which obtain stories or material evidence from witnesses before a criminal trial should be put under a legal obligation to notify both prosecution and defence, and stories which are bought from criminals or associates should not be published unless accompanied by a full statement of the amount of the payment. These laws would not strike against press freedom, but would tend to further the public right to know. Its right, that is, to know the truth about the behaviour of newspapers' editors in situations where editors are demonstrably reluctant to admit the truth to the Press Council.

The Right of Reply

The Press Council has repeatedly asserted the principle that an individual who is personally attacked in a newspaper is entitled to have his or her response to that attack published by means of a letter to the editor, or by a quoted response in a follow-up story, or by the newspaper itself agreeing to a clarification or correction. In 1982 the chairman stated the rule:

> The Council has by a long series of decisions established the principle that in general any person or organisation identifiably attacked in the columns of a newspaper or periodical is morally entitled to, and should be given the opportunity to, make a reasonable reply (which may constitute a correction or explanation) whether by letter or statement published editorially. It must be confined to the subject matter of the attack and be reasonable both in content and in length. [22]

If this principle were consistently applied and obeyed, the 'Right of Reply' legislation promised by the Labour Party would not be necessary. However, the council's adjudications on this point suggest that the right of reply principle which it describes does not coincide with the principle which it applies. The adjudications show that editors may avoid the 'moral duty' to publish a response in a number of ways. These adjudications are not always consistent, but they have held that no right of reply arises in the following circumstances:

● *If the attack is contained in the report of a speech by a third party.* The right of reply only operates when the newspaper itself does the attacking. In other words, a newspaper may headline an entirely unfounded or distorted allegation (perhaps made on a privileged occasion, and hence immune from libel action) and refuse to publish any explanation by the victim. Even where the Press Council concedes that a fairer account of the matter would have been achieved by publishing a letter to 'set the record straight', it will not criticize the newspaper for failure to do so if it has merely reported a speech, or comments made in court or in council committee debates.[23] The Press Council defends this approach on the principle that in such cases the dispute is between the complainant and the attacker, and not the newspaper which has published the attack.[24] It follows that the complainant, who cannot in many cases sue for libel, has no redress.

● *If the attack relates to material published by the complainant elsewhere.* Thus a savagely critical book review may not 'morally oblige' the editor of the reviewing paper to provide the author of the book with space to reply.[25]

● *If there is a possibility of a libel action.* Failure to publish a denial of a possibly defamatory allegation is, in this case, 'understandable and justifiable'. For example, the chief constable of West Yorkshire asked the *Sun* to publish his denial of a story that police officers had watched a couple having intercourse in a police cell. The council held that threats of a libel action in relation to the story were sufficient to disentitle him to his right of reply.[26] It has already been pointed out in relation to the legal waiver that it is difficult to understand how publication of a denial could have any effect on a libel action, if one did occur, other than reducing the award of damages the newspaper might have to pay. It would not have amounted to contempt of court, because the action had not been set down for trial.

● *If the complainant has not been personally attacked.* The editor of the *Daily Mirror* was entitled to refuse to publish a letter by Frank Allaun MP complaining about 'misleading propaganda' in its foreign coverage.[27] This ruling is reasonable enough, but it can easily slide into a technical ground for withholding the right, in cases where there is in reality an identity of interest between the person attacked and the person who seeks to reply on his or her behalf. On this ground, for example, the editor of the *Daily Mail* could be exonerated for refusing to publish the letter by Mr Blaine Stothard's fellow teachers, defending him from personal criticism published in that newspaper after his complaint about a cartoon had been upheld by the Press Council.

• *If the letter of reply is 'overlong' or contains defamatory remarks about newspaper employees.* These are easy 'outs' for editors, and they are frequently taken.[28] The council's support for editors who deny the right of reply on these grounds often seems disingenuous. 'Overlong' letters could always be returned to the sender with an invitation to make the point in no more than a stated number of words. 'Defamatory' statements could be edited. Council adjudications commonly permit editors to escape giving a right of reply by claiming that the letter libels their reporters. By 'libels' they usually mean 'criticizes'. In many cases, these criticisms are not actionable, because a person attacked has qualified privilege in law to defame his or her attacker in the course of answering the attack. The Press Council's failure to understand this aspect of the libel law allows opinionated columnists to vent a spleen to which their editors are not 'morally obliged' to allow a response.

• *If the Press Council thinks that the attack is fair.* Three cases from 1978 indicate the council's approach:

(i) The right of reply need not be granted where 'the leading article was a personally worded comment the newspaper was justified in making'. This is the only explanation given for rejecting a complaint that an editor refused to allow the local chairman of an organization to reply to an editorial statement that 'one of their all-but-brown-shirted bully boys made repeated threats of violence against the Press'. The Press Council's explanation is a good example of its unsatisfactory attention to principle. A personally worded comment in an editorial is exactly the sort of statement which the Press Council has held, in other circumstances, calls for a right of reply.[29]

(ii) A man was described in a local newspaper as a 'discredit' to the city and as being involved in 'vicious' behaviour. The newspaper, which had carried without qualms a number of advertisements for the complainant's bookshop, refused him the right of reply. The adjudication was brief: 'The Press Council considers that the article was factually accurate and sees no reason why a reply should have been published in response to this expression of opinion.' The 'reason' which it might have seen was the 'moral entitlement' which it has consistently promised to complainants. This is unqualified by distinctions between 'facts' and 'opinion'.[30]

(iii) A man was described as 'unmagnificent', 'mean-minded' and 'fizzing with phoney moral indignation'. The council

censured the newspaper for refusing a right of reply to these expressions of opinion.[31]

What principle can be deduced from these apparently inconsistent cases? The only principle is that the Press Council will not enforce a right of reply when it agrees with the newspaper's opinion, or at least accepts the facts on which it is based. Complainants in the first two cases were members of the National Front, and the third was the general secretary of a trade union. The council thought the first two comments were fair, and the third open to debate. This is no doubt correct, but the approach is difficult to reconcile with the right of reply as defined by its chairman. It means that the council judges the accuracy of the facts on which the comment is based before it accords the person attacked the right to answer it. In other adjudications, it has refused a right of reply because the complainant has failed to discharge the burden of proving that the newspaper comment was wrong or unfair.[32]

● *If the reply adds nothing to the facts of the debate.* The council endorsed the *Daily Mirror*'s decision against publishing the reply of a Regional Health Authority to a John Pilger article. It ruled: 'The headline and article were emotive but the subject was emotional . . . the letter did not attempt to make any factual correction but expressed a contrary opinion in terms somewhat abusive to the policy of the newspaper and reporter concerned.'[33] Since it was admittedly an emotional subject, any reply would necessarily express a 'contrary opinion' and be 'somewhat abusive' to those who had been extremely abusive to the Health Authority in a front-page splash report. This is another example of a council adjudication failing to give a reasoned or reasonable basis for the finding. Such a basis did exist, on the facts, because a Health Authority spokesman had been quoted in reply in the body of the original article.

● *If the right of reply has been refused, and the would-be respondent seems to have acquiesced.* An editor will not be criticized for refusing the right of reply if the complainant (however reluctantly, and however wrong the refusal) appears to accept it. The BBC 'Panorama' team was accused of 'cheque-book journalism' and stage-managed sensationalism ('BBC Paid Soccer Maniacs') by the *News of the World*. The 'Panorama' editor, Christopher Capron, wrote a letter denying the allegations, which the newspaper refused to publish on the grounds that it was 'untrue and defamatory'. Mr Capron took no further action, although his producer and reporter complained to the

Press Council that, amongst other things, the newspaper had not given a right of reply. The council held that the 'Panorama' editor 'might have been entitled to complain but he did not pursue it and appeared to accept the rejoinder that he received from the paper'.[34] Either the paper was correct in making that rejoinder or it was not, and in the latter case it deserved censure.

● *If it is not recognizable as an express attack, only an attack by implication.* An example of this exception is provided by a major *Sunday Times* investigation – 'Dirty Tricks in an Ivory Tower' – which demonstrated how an apparently objective academic study of human rights was funded from South Africa for propaganda purposes. A two-column photograph of the study's British editorial assistant, Winifred Crum-Ewing, was published with the story. The implication was that Mrs Crum-Ewing was either a stooge or a dupe of the forces of apartheid, but this was never actually spelled out although she was quoted at some length in the piece. The editor refused to publish a letter by Mrs Crum-Ewing which defended her professional integrity without dissenting from the facts in the article. The Press Council upheld the editor:

> Mrs Crum-Ewing claimed that 'a contentious article entitles the one aggrieved by it to a right of reply'. The Press Council's opinion is that when the complainant has been personally attacked or criticized an opportunity to reply should be given. In this case the *Sunday Times* was entitled to challenge the integrity of the publication and did not go beyond allowable comment on Mrs Crum-Ewing's role in it.[35]

This is a confused adjudication. No reasonable person would interpret the article as other than a reflection on the complainant's integrity or intelligence in allowing herself, wittingly or not, to be a party to 'dirty tricks' of a sort which would be deplored by the majority of *Sunday Times* readers. The article was an outstanding piece of investigative journalism, and to say that the newspaper was 'entitled' to publish 'allowable' comment is an otiose statement of fact which in no way meets the point of the complaint. The purpose of the right of reply, as defined by the council, is to allow people who have been criticized, whether justly or not, to *explain* themselves, and not merely to dispute statements of fact. The case is a good example of the Press Council detracting from its own principles on spurious grounds. There were good reasons for rejecting this complaint on other grounds (the letter added nothing to the points made by the complainant when quoted in the original article, and the complainant apparently attached a confusing condition to publication of her letter). Unfortunately, the Press Council decided the case on a distinction between a 'person aggrieved' and a 'person attacked' which the particular facts did not justify.

• *If the right of reply is overridden by the right to be partisan.* A newspaper is not obliged to give a right of reply to editorials which express its editor's moral or political beliefs, even if such expression includes a powerful and partisan attack on identified or identifiable organizations.

The *Leicester Mercury,* in an editorial headed 'Not in Our Columns', deplored the existence of a homosexual counselling service in Leicester, made reference to paedophilia, and concluded that the activities of homosexual counselling services were not proper to report in a family newspaper and would therefore be denied space. Leicester's only homosexual counselling service, 'Gayline', asked to be allowed to reply in a letter disassociating themselves from paedophilia and explaining that they were a help group, not 'militant' or 'campaigning' homosexuals. The editor told the council of his belief that homosexuals were 'not a responsible social group', and that 'homosexualism was an unnatural practice abhorrent to most people', associated with 'perverted interest in children'.

The adjudication entirely supported the editor. 'There is no absolute right of reply,' it said, to controversial or partisan comment. Individuals had not been identified in the editorial, and

. . . the Editor was entitled to express the strong view he held. It was a matter of discretion for him to decide whether, having regard to what he considered the moral issues involved, he should provide a platform for those taking a different view. The Press Council does not consider that in the circumstances of this case his discretion was exercised in a way that was open to legitimate attack. The complaint against the *Leicester Mercury* is rejected.[36]

The facts of this case show that the adjudication is inconsistent with the chairman of the Press Council's statement (published in the same Annual Report) that 'any organisation identifiably attacked . . . is morally entitled to, and should be given the opportunity to, make a reasonable reply'. Of course the editor was 'entitled' to publish his views, but that is not the point. Those views attacked an identifiable organization, which sought, not a 'platform', but merely to correct errors of fact and emphasis. The intellectual poverty of this particular adjudication is revealed by contrasting it with an adjudication coincidentally issued by the Australian Press Council in the same year (1978) on virtually the same facts. A local newspaper in the northern Queensland city of Townsville had editorially attacked a new homosexual organization which sought to change the law, describing it as 'dedicated to propagation of practices which are reprehensible, against the order of nature and morally degenerative'. The editorial stated that no publicity whatsoever would be given to the group, and refused it a right to reply to the editorial. The council upheld the group's complaint on this principle:[37]

> The Australian Press Council, while re-affirming that a news-paper which purports to serve the general public has the right to advocate any point of view it thinks proper on a question of public controversy, emphasizes the duty of such a paper, when it has published arguments favouring one point of view on such a question, to give reasonable publicity to countervailing arguments.

It went on to apply the principle to the facts of the case, with a logic and vigour so often lacking in its British equivalent:

> The *Townsville Daily Bulletin* is a paper of general news coverage. The Council is clearly of the opinion that such a paper, while within its rights in condemning in the terms of the editorial the proponents of reform of the law on the relevant topic, is under a strong obligation as a matter of ordinary fairness to hold its columns open to a reasonable reply.
>
> The *Bulletin*'s refusal to do this was not only an act of suppression and intolerance, it was a rejection of the duty, which must be accepted if freedom of the Press is to retain the support of the public, to respect the right of the general reader to be informed of the arguments on each side of a public debate upon which a paper has expressed its own views in favour of one point of view.

In many areas, there is only one local newspaper. Editors who take an exceptional, and perhaps eccentric, dislike to a local organization may run a campaign against it, designed perhaps to 'run it out of town', without providing the opportunity for a reasoned response, either to members of the organization attacked or to members of the reading public who write to complain of bias and distortion in the press campaign (such persons, not being personally attacked, do not qualify for a right of reply). The British Press Council, by relying upon editorial discretion and the right to be partisan, thereby leaves the door open for one-sided propaganda campaigns.

• *If reply is sought to editorial comment attached to an earlier reply.* In a number of cases the council has upheld the editor's right to affix a comment to any critical letter. This can range from 'we stand by our original story', to disputing in some detail the correspondent's claims. It has further upheld the editor's discretion to decide that 'correspondence on this matter is now closed' should the correspondent concerned wish to dispute the editorial comment on his or her letter. In other words, there is no right of reply to an editorial reply to a right of reply to an editorial. Inevitably, these rulings give an editor the upper hand by allowing the editor the last word. Editors must be in a position to defend themselves or their reporters against imputations on their integrity, and to point out demonstrable factual errors in published correspondence. But the 'right of reply' is devalued if it is published alongside a scornful rejoinder. If an editor is minded to make such a rejoinder, in fairness its proposed contents should be communicated to the complainant, so the latter has an opportunity to redraft the reply or to withdraw it.

In general, the Press Council's rulings on the right of reply lack coherence and often fail to accord with its own statement of the existence of the right. Some of the qualifications of the right which can be extrapolated from its decisions are justifiable, but some are not. There are other issues which must be addressed before the right can be comprehensively stated: should it only apply to papers which publish daily or weekly news, and not to journals of opinion? Should it be available to political parties? At present, the council offers not so much a right as a generalized assertion of principle, applied inconsistently and arbitrarily. Understandably, it has won no more than lip-service from newspaper editors. In the council's last published report, for 1979, newspapers censured for refusing the right of reply included the *Daily Telegraph* (twice), the *Daily Express* (twice), the *Daily Mirror* and the *Sunday Times*.[38] The council's failure to find a satisfactory formula has had two unfortunate consequences.

Industrial action to demand a right of reply On a number of occasions trade unions have threatened to stop the presses of particular newspapers when editors have refused to print union counter-statements to their own partisan editorials about industrial disputes. The Press Council has immediately condemned 'industrial pressure by newspaper workers and trade unions to interfere with the contents of newspapers against the will of their editors', on the ground that they should instead have taken the opportunity to complain to the Press Council about any refusal of their right of reply to the editorial. 'Like everyone else they are entitled to the assurance that impartial consideration will be given by the Press Council to any complaint by individuals, chapels or unions about a newspaper's content or conduct.'[39] The Press Council does not point out that this consideration will probably take at least six months, by which time the controversy to which the editorial was directed will almost certainly have been settled. Nor does it explain that it is doubtful whether the council will assert a union's right of reply to an editorial, even if the reply is written by union members who work for the paper. As we have seen, this right is subject to the editor's discretion to be partisan, to make comments which the council considers fair, to reject overlong letters, to deny a reply to individuals who are not personally attacked, and to add comment or criticism to any counter-statement published. The assurance of 'impartial consideration' may be hollow, where it appears from the council's own case-law that the complaint is likely to be rejected. In most cases of print-union action, reply had been sought to the newspaper's criticisms of the trade-union side of industrial disputes outside the newspaper industry (e.g. in 1982 the ASLEF dispute and the health workers' pay claim). The council would not, at least according to some of its previous adjudications, uphold the right of a print union to reply in these circumstances, both because the print union is not itself under attack and because the editor is entitled to be partisan.

The council is right to be concerned about cases where newspaper workers refuse to print editions because the editor has refused to give space for them to reply to editorials or articles with which they disagree. The council condemns this censorship, although others are inclined to see it as the only mechanism available to workers to enforce a right which the council promises but cannot deliver. Charles Wintour, ex-editor of the *Evening Standard* and a former member of the council, sees print-union action as 'a crude, brutal and unacceptable form of censorship, but the snail's pace at which the Press Council currently proceeds is bound to lead to occasional explosions. For print workers there sometimes must seem to be no other immediate remedy open than the threat of industrial action.' He goes on to make a point which the council, in its public condemnations of print-union action, has been inclined to ignore:

> In any case it is surely wrong to say that someone who helps to manufacture a product has no more responsibility for it than a casual customer. Manufacturers are continually urging their employees to take a livelier interest in their work. Doesn't this apply to newspaper production workers also?[40]

If the Press Council wishes to act as intermediary in cases of conflict over the right of reply between unions and management, it must give some weight to Wintour's approach. It would be necessary to find a formula which locates a point at which persistent partisanship by a newspaper of one side of an industrial dispute, combined with a refusal to publish any opposing view, would oblige the editor to give workers on that newspaper reasonable space to express disagreement with editorial policy. The council would also need to establish an emergency procedure for dealing with such cases in a matter of days rather than months.

Legislation Another consequence of the Press Council's failure to offer a satisfactory right of reply has been an increasing demand for legislation on the subject. Such legislation works in most Western European countries, and a law to achieve it in Britain has been promised by the Labour Party. A draft Bill has been introduced into parliament on several occasions by Frank Allaun MP, and it very narrowly failed to obtain a second reading in February, 1983. As presently drafted, the Allaun Bill would give a right of reply by obliging newspapers, on pain of a £40,000 fine, to publish counter-statements by companies and organizations of equal length to reports which are alleged to be 'distorted'. Thus, no editor could give substantial space to investigative reporting or campaigning journalism about business or politics without the prospect of providing equal space for an extended reply. One might anticipate that, under this regime, half of the *New Statesman* would be devoted to replies by the National Front, the CBI and the Conservative Party, while half of the *Spectator* would be responses from the National Front, the

TUC and the Labour Party. There are valuable features of the Allaun Bill, but on its wider shores break legal waves which could engulf investigative journalism. Until the Press Council issues a definitive statement of the principle of the right of reply, and places itself in a position to enforce it within a few days of the publication of the original article, statutory measures like the Allaun Bill will continue to have a natural attraction for politicians of all parties.

Privacy

The Press Council has also published a Declaration of Principle on the subject of privacy, the nub of which is as follows: 'The publication of information about the private lives or concerns of individuals without their consent is only acceptable if there is a legitimate public interest overriding the right of privacy . . . . The public interest . . . must be a legitimate and proper public interest and not only a prurient or morbid curiosity.' This Declaration has had little impact. Lord Shawcross admitted, in his final report as chairman of the council in 1977, that the tendency to invade personal privacy for stories of no genuine public interest had increased.[41] One reason for the Press Council's ineffectiveness is that invasion of privacy is a subject which needs to be monitored by the council itself, as those who suffer intrusions are unlikely to wish to relive the experience through the long months before a complaint is adjudicated. The argument for monitoring is given more force in privacy cases by the fact that breaches of the Declaration are relatively easy to locate and investigate. Pictures and stories which detail the romantic entanglements or private griefs of people who are not public figures are published with regularity, but whether they receive the censure they deserve will often depend on whether a public-spirited individual (such as Penelope Money-Coutts – see p. 49) or a local welfare organization is sufficiently appalled to overcome the obstacles of the complaints procedure. In 1979 a fairly typical splash story about a church deaconess who set up home with a parishioner received the council's severest condemnation:

> It particularly deplores the identification of relatives of the couple involved including a schoolchild, as a gross invasion into their privacy which cannot be justified on the grounds of public interest . . . the *Romford Observer* acted irresponsibly

in involving innocent parties, using pictures to denigrate innocent people, and improperly criticized the Vicar editorially. . . .[42]

The *Romford Observer* appears to be distinguished from some other local, and certain national Sunday, newspapers only in the respect that its story became the subject of a complaint to the council by angry parishioners.

The Press Council has shown vigilance in its efforts to protect members of the Royal Family. It has even met in emergency session to condemn the hounding of Prince Charles and Lady Diana, and to condemn publication of pictures of the pregnant Princess on a Caribbean beach out of bounds to all but the telephoto lenses of the Fleet Street paparazzi. But its actions have had no effect. The *Sun* did apologize for the incident, taking the opportunity to reprint the controversial pictures to illustrate its apology, under the banner 'THIS IS WHAT THE ROW'S ALL ABOUT FOLKS!' It then proceeded to demonstrate the genuineness of its concern for Royal privacy by selling the pictures to newspapers around the world.[43]

There are numerous other examples of regular defiance of council rulings in the sphere of privacy. It has repeatedly ruled that 'it is neither fair nor acceptable for newspapers to publish detrimental information about a child just because his parents are well-known',[44] yet the expulsion from school or the arrest or merely the interviewing by police of any child of a famous person is inevitably attended by press publicity. In 1980, after Professor Harry Bedson's suicide was partly attributed by the coroner to press harassment after an outbreak of smallpox in his Birmingham University department, the council declared that people under stress as the result of bereavement or involvement in a public crisis should not be put under pressure by the press.[45] In 1981 it upheld a complaint that a newspaper had harassed the family of a child-heart-transplant donor, and directed newspapers to cooperate in arrangements to relieve the cumulative effect of enquiries on people suffering severe personal grief.[46] In 1983, it was driven to conclude that both Peter Sutcliffe's wife and the relatives of his victims 'were harassed by the media ferociously and callously'.[47]

The council has failed to give workable guidance on the 'public interest' exception to its privacy rule. In the Maureen Colquhoun case, for example, it announced that 'members of Parliament are entitled to a degree of protection in their private lives'. Maureen

Colquhoun lost this protection because she was an MP 'who has taken a very strong stand on feminist issues'.[48] The public was therefore 'entitled' to know that she was sharing a house with another woman. Since this seems perfectly consistent with feminism, wherein lies the genuine interest of the sort which might have been aroused had she taken up residence with a notorious male chauvinist? Had she been hitherto a supporter of the conventional family, with no interest in feminism, would the council really have found no public interest in the story? The adjudication was a matter of public interest because it was 'capable of affecting the performance of her public duties'. If this is the test, then clearly MPs (and other public figures) have no right of privacy at all. Any private or family matter is *capable* of affecting public performance; the correct test for publication should be whether there is reasonable evidence that it has *in fact* affected ability to do a public job.

Privacy is the one area where Press Council adjudications have received recent and independent analysis. Raymond Wacks, a law lecturer and the author of a book on the protection of privacy in English law, argues that the council's Declaration of Principle is an inadequate substitute for a detailed and enforceable statutory code. In his view,

> . . . if the Council is prepared to accept a role of general oversight, the existence of a code is the very least that the public, let alone the Press, is entitled to expect . . . . [Press Council] rulings leave much to be desired. Usually terse and without argument, they are often difficult to understand. What, for instance, is to be understood by an adjudication which declares that a newspaper is 'seriously at fault', but finds that the complaint is 'not substantiated'? What is meant by a decision in which the publicity concerned is 'deprecated' but which then finds that 'no harm' was done by the newspaper? Has the Council 'found for' the newspaper or not? If it is seriously at fault or guilty of conduct to be deprecated, why is the newspaper not censured? There is little elegance in the Council's rulings. How are apparently conflicting decisions to be reconciled? Do later adjudications overrule the reasoning (if any) of earlier ones? . . . The Council evidently convinced the Younger Committee on Privacy that although no statement of principles or code of conduct has been produced, its adjudications 'have been widely promulgated so that editors and journalists have ample precedent to guide them'.

It is hard to perceive what guidance these precedents offer, and even if editors and journalists are thereby better informed, what of the public? . . . Self-discipline is not to be disparaged, but the matter of Press freedom is surely too important to be left to the Press alone. The creation of a statutory Press Council vested with the power to fine or suspend newspapers and journalists and the formulation of a strict code of conduct would improve the existing machinery.[49]

This final solution would certainly improve the protection of privacy, but at the cost of establishing a government-appointed body with the power to punish individual journalists. Some countries favour a legal right to privacy, enforceable in the courts, which can compensate victims by awards of damages. This solution too has drawbacks: ordinary people whose private lives are inexcusably 'exposed' often lack either the money or the knowledge to sue, and trials can be counter-productive by giving dramatic publicity to the original wrong. A more satisfactory answer could be found in a council prepared to build up, through rulings on individual cases, a practical guide for editors and working journalists. It would need additional resources to monitor newspapers, to call for explanations of apparent invasions of privacy (whether they had been complained of or not), to order prominent publication of its adjudications, and in bad cases – where the victim has suffered quantifiable damage – to award compensation. Only in this way can Declarations of Principle pass from the airy realm of counsels of perfection to become practical rules of thumb.

Investigating Ethics

There is little evidence to justify the view that the Press Council's rulings on ethical standards are 'respected, feared and obeyed' by British newspapers. The unsatisfactory quality of the standards it promulgates, its lack of any power to give its rulings a persuasive deterrent force, and the commercial pressures on editors and journalists to seek sensation are some of the factors which have militated against Press Council rulings achieving the impact of a regulatory code. The question of enforcement of council rulings is addressed in the last chapter of this book; the evidence and analysis of the council's handling of public complaints and its formulation of professional standards set out in this chapter and the last indicates that the defects in its existing procedures for investigating complaints constitute serious obstacles to the formulation of acceptable rules. Unless its adjudications are respected, there is little point in enforcing them.

The chief obstacle to the coherent development of professional standards is the council's refusal to monitor the performance of the press. In all but exceptional cases the onus is placed on individual members of the public to come forward and discharge the heavy burden of proving that a particular newspaper has breached a rule – a rule, moreover, which complainants must generally formulate for themselves. This is a hit-or-miss approach to the business of setting standards, based on the wishful thinking that a coherent code will emerge from adjudications on instances, isolated in themselves, which some individual has had either the personal motive or public spirit to bring to the council's attention, and to maintain that attention over many months of the adjudicating process. Lord Devlin once compared the Press Council's approach to the method used by 'generations of judges who produced the common law of England'.[50] That may be so, and the tangle that they made of the common law by their case-precedent approach has required the constant attention of parliament and the Law Commission in order to reduce the common-law jungle to a more orderly system of statute law. If the council's rulings are to be respected, they must be based on rules – worked out in a coherent statement of principles and exceptions, and applied across the board and not as the spirit moves individual members of the public.

These strictures do not apply, at least in theory, to the rare occasions on which the council holds a major enquiry. Every few years, in response to public clamour or judicial criticism over what appears to be a particularly gross breach of professional standards, the council conducts its own investigations and issues a report evaluating press behaviour and setting out the ethical principles involved. Its most celebrated effort in this respect was its report on 'Press Conduct in the Sutcliffe Case'. The delay, deception, and lack of expertise which attended preparation of this report exposed the inadequacies of the council's investigatory procedures, on a subject which exclusively occupied one complaints committee for a period of almost two years.

Press conduct in the Sutcliffe case was an awkward matter to investigate, both for newspapers and for the Press Council. Nothing less than a thorough-going and authoritative report would satisfy the public that the council's system of self-regulation could provide a satisfactory measure of deterrence to the payment of 'blood money'. In order to establish the facts, the council – having no investigative powers or personnel – had to rely upon the full and honest cooperation of editors and executives. A commission of enquiry would have had statutory powers to subpoena documents and to cross-examine witnesses: the council had to rely upon respect. A number of leading newspapers – those with most to hide about their dealings with witnesses and with the Sutcliffe family – failed to provide the cooperation the council required to establish the truth. They did not formally refuse to assist, but adopted policies of withholding vital evidence and sending evasive and misleading replies to council enquiries.

That the Sutcliffe enquiry succeeded at all was largely due to chance. A number of newspapers had denied outright any attempts to make deals with the Sutcliffes. The council was obliged to accept these denials. It happened, however, that one newspaper – the *Daily Mail* – had mentioned, in the course of a self-serving editorial, the fact that its assistant editor had written to Mrs Sutcliffe's solicitor stipulating that the condition of any deal with her would be that a 'substantial proportion' of the payment would have to be made over to the relatives of her husband's victims. Here was a document which, on the *Mail's* own admission, clearly existed, and the council asked to see the office copy of the letter. The *Mail* replied that the copy had, unaccountably, gone missing. So the council wrote to Mrs Sutcliffe's solicitor, Kerry Macgill, asking whether he could produce the original. Solicitors are generally bound by rules of confidentiality in their dealings on behalf of clients: that confidence, however, reposes in the client, and Mrs Sutcliffe agreed to waive it. In consequence, in April 1982 Macgill sent his entire file of newspaper dealings to the Press Council: a file which contained letters, draft contracts, and handwritten notes pushed under the door of the house where Mrs Sutcliffe had taken shelter in the days following her husband's arrest. The existence of these documents had not, for the most part, been disclosed by the newspapers on whose behalf they had been written. The following newspapers were involved:

The Daily Express[51] On 23 June 1981 the editor assured the council that 'no money was offered' to Mrs Sutcliffe. On 14 July 1981 he repeated that 'We did not offer any money whatsoever. We had no intention of making any payment. It has never been the policy of the *Daily Express* to pay money to criminals or their relatives.' The Macgill file, sent to the council nine months later, disclosed:

● On 6 January 1981 a *Daily Express* reporter joined in an offer to Mrs Sutcliffe of £50,000 for an interview.

● A few hours later, another *Express* man offered, on behalf of the paper, 'at least £80,000' for an exclusive story.

● The next day, the deputy news editor wrote confirming the £80,000, but adding 'this does not represent our final offer'.

● Two days later, the editor himself wrote a long letter to Macgill, stating, in the context of rival bids for his client's story, 'we will be happy to discuss any arrangement you may wish to make'.

The council sent copies of these letters to the editor, 'inviting his comments'. His comment, in a written reply some months later, was that he had 'forgotten' about these dealings. The council, understandably, found 'such a lapse of memory astonishing', and 'deplored' the attempt which had been made to mislead it. That attempt had, of course, only been revealed by the fortuitous circumstance of Macgill handing over his file. But for that event, the *Express* would have escaped all censure.

News of the World[52] This newspaper initially assured the council, through its legal manager and long-time Press Council member Henry Douglas, that it had not paid and would not pay any money to Mrs Sutcliffe. The Macgill file disclosed:

● A letter to Macgill from the editor of the newspaper, on 7 January 1981, indicating it was 'prepared to pay a substantial fee' for an exclusive story.

● A letter from Rosalie Shann dated 7 April 1981 requesting an exclusive interview on behalf of the paper, and pointing out 'there would obviously be a considerable amount of money involved'.

● A letter dated 27 April to Macgill from the assistant editor, offering Mrs Sutcliffe 'a fee of not less than £110,000' and 'a seat at the editor's desk' while the story was prepared, together with travel and accommodation for herself and her family during the trial.

● An undated letter from the newspaper, enclosing a fully prepared contract, in anticipation of an exclusive story told 'entirely in her own words . . . assisted by Rosalie Shann, one of the most caring and compassionate writers in journalism'.

The Press Council duly sent these documents to the editor,

inviting his response. It came, as usual, from Henry Douglas, who 'said he was instructed, after taking advice, that they should not enter into any correspondence with the Council about the letters'. Indeed, the council had no business reading the letters in the first place: 'In their (i.e. *News of the World*'s) opinion, letters written to [Mrs Sutcliffe's] lawyers and through him to her should not have been disclosed to a third party, the Press Council.' The council pointed out, in its adjudication, that 'If the Press Council is to discharge its duty to investigate press conduct and maintain press standards it must not only have access to such material but be able to make such use of it as the Council finds necessary.' It 'regrets the lack of candour' shown by the *News of the World* in failing to disclose 'highly relevant' evidence.

The Yorkshire Post[53] The editor assured the council that no payments were made to Mrs Sutcliffe. The Macgill file revealed several letters making implicit offers, one of them estimating that the price could be as high as £1 million. The council accused the editor of attempting to mislead it by an 'incomplete' reply which lacked candour.

The Daily Mail[54] This newspaper assured the Press Council that a decision not to pay Mrs Sutcliffe had been made four days after the arrest, and adhered to thereafter. However, merely to 'keep the lines of communication open', a letter had been written to Macgill indicating that a precondition of any deal would have to be the payment of a 'substantial proportion' of royalties to relatives of Sutcliffe victims. The council asked for a copy of the letter, but was told it could not be found. The Macgill file disclosed a considerable amount of detailed correspondence with the *Daily Mail,* continuing for three months after the decision not to pay Mrs Sutcliffe had been taken. It included a retraction of the 'substantial proportion' condition, a detailed draft contract, references to 'high five-figure sums' and offers which would go even higher, and a written assurance by the newspaper's assistant editor that 'in the long term such an arrangement could only benefit Mr Peter Sutcliffe'. There was even a letter from the newspaper's legal adviser, written in 1982, setting out his interpretation of phrases in the correspondence and offering to pay Macgill for the time he might care to spend clarifying matters. The editor, David English, refused to attend an oral hearing of the complaints committee at which he would have had to answer questions from the person who initiated a specific complaint against the *Mail*, Mrs Doreen Hill (mother of a Sutcliffe victim). Sir David's reason was that 'emotions would get out of hand and it would be distressing for Mrs Hill and himself'.

The council, in its adjudication, 'regretted' Sir David's refusal to attend an oral hearing with Mrs Hill, who had behaved impeccably when attending a hearing with another newspaper editor against whom she had lodged a complaint. It stated that it had been 'hampered' in its consideration of the matter by the *Mail*'s failure to disclose material of obvious relevance to the enquiry. It accepted the editor's word, supported by the newspaper's executives (one of whom, at the time of its report, was vice-chairman of the Press Council, see p. 24) that the negotiations with Mrs Sutcliffe and her lawyers were an 'elaborate charade' designed to spoil the plans of rival newspapers and perhaps to obtain her story without payment. The newspaper was censured for 'gross misconduct' for its sustained deception.

The Daily Star[55] The fact that the *Daily Star* had paid £4000 to the woman with Sutcliffe at the time of his arrest was revealed at his trial. The *Star* had therefore no option but to admit to this payment, although it refused to supply the council with a copy of the contract, stating that this would be a breach of confidence. The council entirely overlooked this refusal to cooperate, and merely censured the newspaper for making payment to a potential witness. A few days after the council's report was published, the *Sunday Times* alleged that the *Star* had not revealed to the council other payments it had made to Peter Sutcliffe's brothers. These allegations were not convincingly denied by the *Star,* and have opened the question of how many payments were made to relatives and friends who were not represented by Macgill, and hence not discovered by the Press Council. The *Star*, incidentally, during the course of the council's enquiries paid Michael Fagan (the Buckingham Palace intruder) £800 and offered him £10,000 for exclusive interviews. One interview appeared in that paper a week before the council's report on Sutcliffe was published.

The Press Council report on the Sutcliffe case was disturbing enough, but it did not get at the whole truth. It was not a proper exercise in investigation or enquiry: witnesses were not interviewed, editors were not cross-examined, newspaper executives were favoured by being allowed to submit their frayed excuses in writing or through a 'legal manager'. The report censured news-papers, but failed to blame the individuals within newspaper organizations who were responsible for criticized decisions – the decisions to mislead the Press Council being arguably more blameworthy than the decisions to pay money to the Sutcliffes. After the report was published, more information came to light. Granada's 'World in Action' programme revealed that the *News of the World* was prepared to offer Sonia Sutcliffe £130,000, a payment personally approved by proprietor Rupert Murdoch.[56] It also produced evidence that the *Daily Star* had paid the Sutcliffe brothers £26,500 for information and services (including the service of spying on sister-in-law Sonia for the *Star*). These payments had been made a few weeks after the *Star*'s editor, Lloyd Turner, had personally called upon Mrs Doreen Hill to assure her of his opposition to payment of blood money to relatives of criminals. 'World in Action' revealed how cheque-book journalism had continued unabated in the weeks after the Press Council report, as newspapers and news agencies offered large sums for photographs of another suspected murderer. After this programme, an abashed Press Council re-opened its Sutcliffe enquiry, to consider the 'new evidence' which had been obtained by simple investigative methods (e.g. sending researchers to confront important witnesses and ask them questions) which the Press Council has been reluctant to adopt.

The council's report, 'Press Conduct in the Sutcliffe Case' is the most impressive effort it has made in its thirty years' history. Yet that report owes such credibility as it does possess to an entirely fortuitous circumstance, namely Mrs Sutcliffe's agreement to waive her rights of confidentiality in her solicitor's file of correspondence with the press. As an investigation, it is an unsatisfactory piece of work: it proceeded for the most part by way of collecting written communications with editors and executives, who were not even cross-examined about the remarkable discrepancies between their initial claims and the evidence in the Macgill file. Their conduct was 'regretted', it 'lacked candour', but under a more searching investigation, those gentle rebukes might well have been much harsher. Confronted with the evidence of how little its requests for information met with responses conditioned by respect, fear and obedience, the council could only caution: 'If newspapers fail to disclose voluntarily documents which are obviously relevant to complaints made against them they will have only themselves to blame if some statutory power is introduced to compel the production of such documents.'[57]

A statutory power to compel the disclosure of documents in newspaper offices is a draconian remedy. It would inspire a new breed of complainants – those who would seek the council's assistance, not for the correction of mistakes, but in order to fish for the sources for information which had been published about them. A more satisfactory alternative would be for the council to arm itself, by contracts with its own subscribers, with power to call for relevant information, subject to appropriate safeguards to protect sources and to withhold genuinely confidential information. Whenever a newspaper is caught out in a breach of that duty, the proprietor should suffer the indignity, not of a polite regret, but of a fine imposed by a penalty clause in the contract. An enquiry as fundamental and far-reaching as that into press misconduct in the Sutcliffe case should not have been carried out by the council at all, but rather by a judicial enquiry with full powers to call for, and to test, the evidence. The necessity for such a drastic step after the next sensational case would be eliminated if parliament adopted the simple expedient of requiring newspapers to reveal the nature of any payment made to friends, relatives and associates of criminals (see above).

The Press Council enquiry into the Sutcliffe case was announced on 7 January 1981. Its report was published on 4 February 1983. The council seeks to explain the delay on the grounds of sub judice. It points out that Sutcliffe's appeal was dismissed in May 1982, and not until the autumn of that year did it 'learn from the Attorney General that the possibility of an appeal by Mr Sutcliffe to the House of Lords no longer stood in the way of publication of this report'.[58] In fact, Sutcliffe's appeal never stood in the way of publication of the report. That appeal was based entirely upon the trial judge's treatment of the medical evidence; it raised no issue remotely affecting, or affected by, the Press Council's enquiry. The council's explanation for the delay lacks candour. It did not even get around to writing to Macgill to ask him for the *Daily Mail* letter until April 1982 – after its 'investigation' had been in progress for fifteen months.[59]

5
Freedom of the Press

According to its constitution, the first object of the Press Council is to preserve the established freedom of the British Press.

The first Royal Commission on the Press, reporting in 1949, was surprised that the industry had no coherent mechanism for self-defence, and foresaw the 'General Council of the Press', which it proposed, speaking out powerfully against attempts to erode freedom of expression and information. The need for such a body is much greater now than it was in 1949: there has over the last decade been a veritable explosion of legislation and common law affecting, and to some degree restricting, the media in Great Britain. A body with the stated objectives of the Press Council should have been in the vanguard of the forces opposing these developments. In fact, it has been largely irrelevant.

What might the council's first objective entail? A duty to preserve an established freedom implies a responsibility for taking positive action against any legislative or judicial initiative to cut back that freedom by restraining the press from entering an area previously open to it, or by using the law – criminal or civil – to suppress information or to chill investigative reporting. Thus the Press Council would seem to have a duty under its own constitution to *monitor* impending legislation, to *publicize* aspects of that legislation inimical to press freedom; to *publish* its concern as widely as possible; to *lobby* parliamentarians, and to *rally* support in opposition to the proposals. Moreover, it should take positive steps to seek reform of the law to the advantage of the press, by encouraging and sponsoring desirable legislative initiatives. Where setbacks to press freedom come, as they often do, through an adverse court decision, its duty would be to explain to the public the dangers of that decision, to support appeals against it (if necessary to the European Court of Human Rights) and to encourage legislation which would overturn it. Both objectives appear to require the council to keep the law under constant scrutiny, and publicly to call the bluff of those who would use it to censor, injunct or punish public-interest reporting.

There have been times when the Press Council has lived up to the first object of its charter. Its proudest achievement was in 1966, after the Attorney General, supported by the Prime Minister, had stated in parliament that newspapers might be charged with contempt if they interviewed witnesses to the Aberfan disaster (a landslide in Wales which killed many schoolchildren) before a Tribunal of Enquiry had deliberated. The Council issued an immediate statement declaring that the government's threat was too sweeping, and that the press was entitled to conduct the interviews. Coming from Lord Devlin, the council's declaration had a magisterial ring, and was followed by a booklet setting out the legal rights of reporters and calling for an official enquiry into the application of contempt law to government tribunals.[1] Such an enquiry was duly established, under Lord Justice Salmon, and it largely vindicated the council's stand.[2] Subsequently, the council presented polished evidence in defence of press freedom to the Younger Committee on Privacy and the Faulks Committee on Defamation, and published that evidence in persuasive pamphlets.[3]

The response of the council to these issues in more recent years has lacked spirit and resource. It is as though the desire to preserve its image as a complaints body independent of the press has sapped its will to speak out on behalf of the press against encroachments on press freedom. It has done little more than to issue occasional short press statements criticizing aspects of the law of contempt or official secrecy. Welcome as these may be, they contribute nothing to reform movements, which require continual research, lobbying and provision of information. The council's reaction to recent developments may be judged from the following examples.

The attempt to brand journalists as spies In 1977 the Attorney General launched the most oppressive prosecution against journalists in recent history. He sanctioned the use of Section 1 of the Official Secrets Act (which carries up to fourteen years' imprisonment), a law which had formerly only been deployed against spies and saboteurs, in an attempt to put behind bars two young journalists, Duncan Campbell and Crispin Aubrey, who had interviewed a former soldier. The prosecution opposed bail for both men at several stages prior to the trial. The use of Section 1 against investigative journalists with no contacts with foreign powers was manifestly excessive, and was designed to remove important areas of the Defence establishment from public scrutiny. This 'ABC' trial, as it became known, took place in 1978, and the Section 1 charges were pursued by the government. They were only dropped at the insistence of the judge, who said in mid-trial that they were 'oppressive'.[4]

In its report for the year 1978, published in July 1981, the Press Council found an opportunity to mention the ABC trial. It described it as a 'charade' and as a 'long running farce'.[5] Neither journalist found it particularly amusing at the time, and neither was given the slightest support, moral or financial, by the Press Council. They heard nothing from the council from the time of their arrest. In 1981 the council found it safe to say what it should have shouted, loudly and clearly, at the government three years before. It was apparent from the outset that these journalists were not spies for any foreign power, yet the council made no protest as the law officers sought to extend the law designed for traitors to trap investigative journalists. A firm and timely statement from the Press Council in 1977, relating to the proper scope of Section 1, need not have amounted to contempt, nor would a decision by it to support the journalists' defence have done so. The Press Council remained silent until this attempt to destroy one 'established freedom' of the press had long since passed.

The ABC case gave rise to the 'Colonel B' affair. The colonel was the chief prosecution witness in the case, and his name was said to be a top secret, although journalists easily discovered it from public sources. The magazines which published it were prosecuted for contempt, whereupon several MPs contrived to mention it in parliament. That was the cue for the Attorney General to make a heavy-handed attempt to threaten the press if it dared to use its 'established freedom' to report the parliamentary proceedings. The Press Council took no action to condemn this threat, or to support *The Leveller, Peace News* and the NUJ itself in their prosecution for contempt.[6] Three years after the contempt convictions were quashed by the Law Lords, the council saw fit to refer, for the first time, to 'the Colonel "B" fiasco'.[7]

Freedom of Information Act From time to time the Press

Council issues short press statements welcoming or calling for moves to introduce a Freedom of Information Act. It does nothing further, however, to promote or to lobby for such legislation. In 1978 a private member's Bill on this subject was introduced by Clement Freud, given a second reading and actually passed through eleven committee stages before it lapsed with the 1979 election. To push a complicated and controversial legislation so far, without government support, was a magnificent effort on behalf of the press.[8] Those who achieved it attest to receiving no assistance whatsoever from the Press Council. The hard work of drafting and lobbying was done by the Outer Circle Policy Unit, a research group sponsored by the Rowntree Trust, with assistance from the National Council for Civil Liberties (NCCL) and individual lawyers and academics. The Press Council confined itself to welcoming the initiative in its report published two years after the initiative had finally foundered.[9]

In 1979 the Conservative government introduced a bill on official secrets, appropriately enough entitled the Protection of Official Information Bill. It was hurriedly withdrawn after publication of *Climate of Treason*, the book which led to the revelation of Anthony Blunt's spying career. This revelation would have been a criminal offence under the provisions of the Bill. The council issued short statements drawing attention to some of the Bill's dangers, and calling upon the government to consult interested parties before making any attempt to reintroduce it.[10] The council itself has made no serious attempts to promote reforms, and in 1981 the Outer Circle Policy Unit closed through lack of funds.

Secrecy laws There are 101 separate Acts of Parliament which threaten civil servants with jail for disclosing to the press quite ordinary information, often about matters of health or safety.[11] For example, factory inspectors who discover that workers are in danger from asbestos poisoning have been threatened with prosecution under S 154 of the Factories Act for divulging unauthorized information. This pile of legislation throws a blanket of secrecy over questions ranging from the safety of workers in abattoirs and nuclear power plants to details of the volume of excrement pumped into sewage farms in Scotland (see Section 50 of the Sewerage [Scotland] Act). Thirty-five of these secrecy laws have been passed by parliament in the last ten years without any opposition from the Press Council or from any other media organization. They have simply not been noticed, because they have taken the form of clauses in legislation which, from its general subject-matter, does not appear to affect free speech. The council may call fitfully for freedom of information; meanwhile, barriers to disclosure are routinely erected to stop public servants revealing to the press details about waste and inefficiency. It is a sad reflection on the media in Britain that no organization exists with sufficient expertise and vigilance to monitor legislation and to provide advance warning of hidden dangers.

'D' Notices and disinformation The Press Council did not give evidence to the Parliamentary Select Committee which in 1980 considered the operation of the 'D' notice system for warning the press about publication of military information.[12] This was another abdication of its claim to promote press freedom, given the opportunity that the enquiry provided for demolishing an archaic system of censorship by wink and nod from the Ministry of Defence. In the end, the case against 'D' notices was propounded by journalists from 'World in Action', the *New Statesman* and the Press Association.

During the Falklands crisis, all sections of the media became furious with the behaviour of the Ministry of Defence. Journalists with the task force were censored, 'minded' and kept away from the action; MOD briefings in London were marked by evasiveness and lack of cooperation, and some British newspapers were fed with false stories and disinformation, apparently in the hope of confusing their Argentinian readers. The press made serious accusations against the Ministry, and the Ministry made serious accusations against the press. The Press Council was not perceived as relevant to the unfolding dispute, and it did not assist the subsequent parliamentary enquiry. The only person who seems to have thought of the Press Council in the context of journalistic coverage of the Falklands was the proprietor of the 'Upland Goose' public house in Port Stanley, who refused to serve drunken correspondents and threatened to report them to the council on the ground that their behaviour was 'worse than the Argies'.[13]

Public records Routine civil-service files generally remain closed to the press for a minimum of thirty years. More embarrassing information can be suppressed for as long as 100 years, and in some cases destroyed entirely. For example, records of field executions in the First World War have been withheld to avoid embarrassment to the Ministry of Defence by exposing the brutality of justice in the trenches; records of Nazi sympathizers and collaborators in the 1930s have been suppressed to avoid embarrassing them in old age; most security-service records have never been released. According to the Public Records Act, the Lord Chancellor's permission is needed before any document can be withheld for more than thirty years, but no guidance is given by the Act as to which documents fall into this special category. The Wilson Report on public records, issued in 1980, described the Lord Chancellor's responsibility as 'little more than a convenient fiction'.[14] It revealed that public servants maintain this fiction by obtaining the Lord Chancellor's approval for blanket bans on *classes* of documents, usually for 100 years. There are now more than forty *classes* of documents which must remain secret for a century.

The civil-service obsession with secrecy is inimical to press freedom, and their use of the Public Records Act to over-classify Whitehall papers is a major reason why public-interest material is withheld from public circulation. Yet the Press Council gave no evidence to the Wilson Committee, and has displayed no sign of even noticing its important recommendations. Wilson proposed the release of more classes of documents *before* thirty years had elapsed, the abolition of 'embarrassment' as a ground for suppression, removal of the civil-service power to keep certain documents secret forever, and a right to appeal against secrecy orders. These recommendations, if implemented, would be a major victory for press freedom. The Press Council has done nothing to support them or bring them to public attention.

The Contempt of Court Act This legislation was before parliament between November 1980 and July 1981. It was a complicated Bill, directly affecting the press, in many ways adversely. Debates were continuously held in parliament over the proper extent of press freedom, and many organizations anxiously lobbied in support. There was no particular lobbying effort by the Press Council. Of the various submissions made to MPs over this Bill, those from press interests were the most inadequate and unconvincing. The best case for media freedom was argued by the Independent Television Companies' Association and the NCCL (both organizations actually sent representatives to attend select committee sessions and to lobby MPs) with worthy support from the Outer Circle Policy Unit and the Law Society.

Nothing of any consequence emanated from the Press Council – no policy, no analysis, no attempt to persuade politicians that the interests of free speech are at least as important as the interests of the legal profession and the courts.

Newspapers are now in a thorough mess over the new Contempt Act. They have discovered that it dampens the comments they may make on cases pending appeal, that it gives courts the power to make wide orders prohibiting or postponing the reporting of evidence, that it impinges upon their coverage of minor tribunals, and that it threatens journalists with jail if they approach a juror after a trial is over. All these restrictions, and more, were apparent for months before the Act came into force, when there was still an opportunity to amend it. The Press Council's finest achievement came when it protected newspapers from threats of contempt after the Aberfan disaster; fifteen years later, when those threats were very much more serious, it took no effective action to combat them. At the very least it could have obtained authoritative legal opinions on the scope of the Bill, and could have organized its constituent bodies into setting up a powerful opposition to the most dangerous clauses. The Contempt Bill was probably the most important single piece of legislation affecting the press since the war; the Press Council's failure to make any contribution to combating its dangers gives reason to doubt whether it is now able or willing 'to preserve the established freedom of the Press'.

Reporting restrictions In 1958, the Press Council was particularly exercised about attempts to restrict the reporting of committal proceedings. It made submissions to the Tucker Commission on the subject, and to the government, arguing strongly against any restraints.[15] It lost the argument – the government finally imposed a prohibition on committal reporting – but it won a minor victory in that the legislation permitted *any one defendant* to lift those restrictions at will. The fruits of this victory were notably enjoyed by the press when one defendant, George Deakin, exercised this right, against the wishes of his co-defendants, in the Thorpe committal at Minehead. Liberal Party lawyers drafted legislation to prevent it from happening again, by giving magistrates the power to override a defendant's choice for publicity if they decide that 'the interests of justice' so require. This legislation – The Criminal Justice (Amendment) Bill – was accepted by all parties, and went through parliament in 1981 without any opposition at all. The Press Council displayed no sign of even noticing it, let alone criticizing it and seeking to arouse opposition. It is extraordinary that a right which the council had struggled to preserve in its early days should be given up without the slightest protest. A piece of established freedom – established in part by the Press Council's own efforts – was virtually destroyed without a murmur from it.

Section 11 of the Prevention of Terrorism Act This Act was passed hurriedly through parliament in the wake of the Birmingham bombings of 1974. It is a 'temporary measure' which has since been renewed every year. Nobody noticed that it affected the press until, five years after its inception, the Attorney General claimed that Section 11 requires journalists who make arrangements to interview representatives of terrorist organizations to inform the security services beforehand. Journalists who fail to do so – even before the interview takes place – could risk up to five years' imprisonment for withholding information which 'might be of assistance' to the apprehension of terrorists. The Press Council did not recognize the dangers in this piece of legislation at the time and has not been disposed either to contest the government's interpretation of the Act or to make any representations for its amendment.

Libel In 1973 the Press Council published its submissions to the Faulks Committee on Defamation, and many of them were accepted when the committee reported two years later.[16] But it has done nothing since to encourage legislation by publicizing the increasingly defective state of the libel law. The reforms recommended by Faulks would have gone some distance towards relieving the press from its most intense legal pressure. They would also, ironically, have protected the Press Council by a statutory extension of the 'qualified privilege' defence to cover reports of its meetings and adjudications. A degree of commitment – a deployment of funds and resources, a constant pressure on parliament – is necessary to obtain reform. The Press Council, while 'in favour' of reform, does little or nothing to achieve it. In 1982, the government announced that it had no current plans for implementing the Faulks's proposals.

Breach of confidence In the past few years, this civil action has been used in attempts to restrain the publication of the Thalidomide saga, the Crossman Diaries, articles about Slater-Walker, a book about MI5, a television documentary ('The

Primados Affair'), *New Statesman* revelations about Australian foreign policy, *City Limits* revelations about British foreign policy, and other material of public interest. The courts have developed the doctrine in certain ways which are inimical to press freedom, and there is a need for the industry to support some Law Commission recommendations, made in 1981, which would help to protect public-interest reporting.[17] British law, whereby any newspaper may be injuncted from publishing confidential documents if the 'balance of convenience' supports the plaintiff, is in marked contrast to American law, where the Supreme Court has held (in the 'Pentagon Papers' case) that the First Amendment prohibits restraint on any publication short of leakage of strategic information in wartime. The Press Council made a submission on the law of confidence to the Law Commission (which recommended a special public-interest defence for the media) but it has not published that submission or used the commission's report to campaign for reform of the law. Breach of confidence is a complex legal subject, and the industry needs an expert organization to give it a lead. The council, which was once active on similarly difficult issues of contempt, libel and court reporting, has failed to acquire the resources or the resolve to lead the press out of the common-law morass that is breach of confidence.

Breach of copyright Copyright is potentially as dangerous a brake on investigative journalism as confidence. The 'public interest' defence to an action for breach of copyright is narrow, and injunctions can be granted if the plaintiff has an arguable case. Large newspaper chains may obtain exclusive property rights in newsworthy photographs, and deny rivals the opportunity to reproduce them. The authors of written documents, and the corporations which employ such authors, may stop newspapers from publishing investigative articles which quote extensively from them, even though the article has a strong public-interest flavour. In 1980, for example, the Government of Australia was allowed to impound all unsold copies of one edition of the *New Statesman*, on the ground that an article quoted some undiplomatic diplomatic cables.

The Press Council has been silent on the subject of copyright. A committee under Mr Justice Whitford sat for several years and reported on the law in 1977; some newspaper publishers gave evidence, but the Press Council ignored it. The committee recommended that the law should be amended to permit the press a greater freedom to criticize and comment upon works of public interest, so long as the comment was not calculated to lower the commercial value of quoted material.[18] It also recommended that staff journalists be given greater rights over the work they produce for their employers. The council mentioned the Whitford Report in a few lines in its 1977 Annual Report (published several years later) but it has done nothing to support (or even to indicate its agreement with) the recommendations.[19] Nor has it passed any comment on the controversy over the monopoly in publication of television schedules possessed by *TV Times* and *Radio Times*, acquired through an unsatisfactory application of the copyright laws. This monopoly denies other newspapers and magazines the freedom to provide readers with a full weekly coverage of television programmes.

Investigating business In 1981 the media lost several important rights to report on business activities, without any protest from the Press Council. The legal obligation on private companies to disclose proper accounts was largely abolished by the 1981 Companies Act, thereby protecting many corporate enterprises from public scrutiny. Some companies were even relieved of their former duty to prepare a profit and loss account and to issue a directors' report, while others (including those with several hundred employees and turnovers amounting to millions of pounds) were relieved from duties of publicizing details of their turnovers.[20] Business journalists were handicapped by these changes, which cut back recently established opportunities for them to obtain information. The Press Council, and other press lobbies for that matter, put up no resistance. In 1977 a Government Green Paper recommended that public companies should be obliged to issue social impact statements, which would give the press information about environmental consequences of company operations, the use of pension funds, application of profits and other potentially illuminating matters.[21] The 1981 Act did not incorporate these recommendations, which have not been supported (or perhaps even noticed) by the Press Council.

Reporting public utilities The rights of media access to meetings of public utilities have also been cut back without apparent Press Council concern. In 1980, local government legislation permitted the establishment of Urban Development Corporations to take over some local-authority duties by promoting the redevelopment of city slum and wasteland; unlike local authorities, however, they may exclude the press from their meetings.[22] In 1983, amendments to the Water Act specifically excluded the press from attendance at meetings of new water authorities, although the public had formerly been entitled to be present. The media must henceforth make do with second-hand reports and publicity handouts about policies concerning pollution and pricing, instead of being present when these important decisions are taken. Thus the 'established freedom of the press' trickles away, usually without protest from a Press Council which has the preservation of that freedom as its first object.

Blasphemy, obscenity and criminal libel When the law of blasphemy was brought back from the dead in 1977 by way of a successful prosecution of *Gay News* over a poem published in its literary section, the Press Council forbore to make any public comment.[23] Yet the minority press deserves the council's support; our 'established freedoms' were mostly established by editors of fringe journals. The Williams Committee on Obscenity sat for over two years without receiving any submission from the Press Council, although the council has considered on several occasions the propriety of national newspapers using four-letter words and publishing prurient articles. The council has not commented upon the committee's recommendation to lift all restraints on the written word.[24] Nor has it made any comment on the Law Commission's proposals, released in 1982, to restrict the scope of the archaic offence of criminal libel.[25]

Other cases The Press Council has withheld comment upon a number of recent cases involving journalistic freedom. It made no protest when *Evening Standard* journalist Mark Hosenball was deported to his native America for unspecified offences, after a procedure which did not give him the right to know, let alone to answer, the allegations made against him. The Press Council confined itself to noting, in its 1977 Annual Report, published several years afterwards, that 'Press and Parliament were concerned'.[26] The council did not protest when former National Council for Civil Liberties solicitor, Harriet Harman, was proceeded against for contempt for showing Home Office documents, read out in open court, to a journalist writing an article about prison policy.[27] The NCCL has been more effective in warning of dangers to press freedom than the Press Council.

There are many other cases affecting press liberty which the Press Council has ignored, save for a brief note in its subsequent Annual Report. One decision which it did criticize, by way of a letter to *The Times* from its director, was *BSC v Granada* (the case of the British Steel 'mole').[28] This action earned a rebuke from Sir James Goldsmith, who argued that the chairman of the council, Mr Patrick Neill QC, should not have appeared in his professional capacity as Granada's advocate, because he thereby became an advocate for the very cause that the council was espousing.[29] This criticism seems misplaced – there was an identity, rather than a conflict, of interests, and Granada's attempt to protect its sources provided an important test case. Indeed, the council should have gone further than merely expressing its view in a letter to *The Times*, by actively supporting the attempt which was made (with partial success) to amend the Contempt Bill to provide protection for journalistic sources.

Police and Criminal Evidence Bill This legislation was published in 1982, and went through its committee stage in the House of Commons in the early months of 1983. It would have been obvious to anyone reading the Bill that Clause 10 gave police special powers to obtain confidential information from journalists, which might include the identity of a source, by applying for a warrant to search their homes or offices for unpublished information. Journalists are protected to some extent by the Contempt Act against being obliged to answer questions about their sources in the witness box; the effect of Clause 10 would be to undermine that protection by allowing police to ransack a journalist's premises in search of information long before any question of giving evidence could arise. The vigilance of organizations claiming a concern for press freedom could be judged by the alacrity of their protests. The NCCL was first off the mark in 1982, and its critical analysis of the Bill prompted the protests which were soon heard from the NUJ. Later, the Law Society and the Guild of British Newspaper Editors added their voices to the chorus. However, it was concern for doctors and priests, rather than journalists, which put most pressure on the government to reconsider. The British Medical Association waged an unrelenting campaign against the Bill with a vehemence which took the government by surprise, and concessions were finally made when the Church of England bishops declared firmly against the clause. In all the clamour, the

Press Council could manage only a belated letter to *The Times* from its director, published on 14 March 1983 – a week after consideration of the clause had been concluded by the House of Commons Committee. The council's response was much too little, and far too late, for its views on the subject to be accorded much weight or relevance.

The Council's Dilemma

The established legal freedom of the British press is under constant threat from both parliament and the courts. A torrent of legislation and case law has brought new restrictions and confinements. The Press Council was established, in part, to organize opposition to such developments and the first object of its constitution imposes upon it a duty so to do. But in recent years it has provided no authoritative leadership on legal matters. Its available resources are largely devoted to processing public complaints.

There may be a connection between the council's lack of activity on press-freedom issues, and its desire to defend its complaints function from public criticism. As the proportion of lay membership on the council has increased to a third (in 1973) and a half (in 1978), so interest in combating restrictive laws seems to have declined. This increasing (and in a consumer context, entirely proper) 'democratization' of the council seems to have changed the way in which it wishes to be publicly perceived. It needs to be trusted by the public to adjudicate complaints *against* the press, and to condemn and censure the press in appropriate cases. It must therefore avoid any suggestion that it is an apologist *for* the press: it must be seen as independent and impartial, a positive scourge of press malpractice. It must not be seen lobbying too hard in favour of press liberty, because that would detract from its posture as an impartial body which condemns press licence. In short, it has allowed its complaints function to overwhelm and obscure its defence function, both in time expended and in its public profile.

This development is understandable, given the degree of comment from the Younger Committee and the third Royal Commission on the need to demonstrate that complaints are adjudicated impartially between press and public. The Royal Commission, indeed, reserved its most scathing strictures for the council's displays of pro-press bias, and pointed out that its 'worthy' objects of defending press freedom 'could be carried out by professional or trade associations'. The commission was firmly of the view that 'the task of considering complaints against the press is the one object for which such a body as the Press Council is essential, and only if it is independent will citizens be satisfied that their interests are being safeguarded'.[30] Complainants against newspapers will not be satisfied that justice has been done, if it is done by an organization which appears to be a wholehearted defender of the press. The difficulties in the council's dual role emerged in the course of its evidence to the third Royal Commission. The commission posed this question:

> What would be the effect on the role and constitution of the Press Council if the function of hearing complaints were to be removed from it to an independent body? Does the Council consider that its role as an adjudicator on complaints strengthens or weakens its role as spokesman for the Press when it feels that the freedom of the Press is threatened?

The council responded:

> It would in the Council's view be extremely unfortunate if the role of hearing complaints were removed to what is described as 'an independent body'. As the Royal Commission will have observed, the first object of the Press Council is the defence of the established freedom of the British Press. The Council is not a commercial or a trade association. It is an organisation devoted to the defence of a *public* right and it is fundamental to the activities of the Press Council and to its independence of the Press in the performance of its duties that it should recognise that freedom is indivisible from responsibility to the public. And that is what the investigation of complaints is all about. Every section of the Council is planned and executed in what the Council conceives to be the public interest. It instantly reacts against being involved in any proposition that smacks of commercial or trade union interest and refers such matters at once to the numerous competent organisations which already exist for such purposes.[31]

While there may be 'numerous competent organisations' to deal with commercial or trade-union issues, there is no organization at present in existence which operates to defend freedom of expression in a powerful way. The council's notion that freedom and responsibility are simply two sides of the same 'public interest' coin is an oversimplification: the most important cases involve a balance between *competing* public interests – the interest in free expression must be weighed against privacy, national security, fair trial and so on. It is time that the public interest in free expression had a full-blooded champion, if only because the other interests have their existing and powerful champions in government and the courts. By adopting the role of arbiter, the Press Council abdicates its first objective, which is 'to defend the established freedom of the British Press', not 'to decide whether the established freedoms conflict with what the council deems to be the public interest, and to defend only those parts which do not'. In this evidence to the Royal Commission, of course, the council is defending the performance of its complaints function against a suggestion that it be removed to an independent body. The defence it offers is the only defence which could be offered against such a proposal – that the council itself acts independently of press interests. But it is a defence which entails the admission that, when free speech conflicts (as it often does) with some other public interest, the council will not necessarily speak out in defence of press freedom. The council can only defend its complaints function by abandoning, or at least revising, the first objective of its constitution.

The council's dilemma is apparent when it moves outside the sphere of ethics and considers whether newspapers should be punished by law. It has gone so far as to set aside its first duty of preserving the established freedom of the press, by encouraging the Attorney General to prosecute newspapers for exercising that freedom. In 1981, the press reported a public and indeed televised conference held by senior Yorkshire police officers who displayed an irresponsible euphoria at the arrest of Peter Sutcliffe. The Attorney General later commented that it would not have been in the public interest to bring contempt prosecutions against the press. The chairman of the Press Council wrote to the Attorney General, inviting him to identify the aspect of the public interest which had weighed against prosecution. The chairman drew to the Attorney General's attention allegations that newspapers had deliberately breached reporting restrictions when Sutcliffe appeared on remand and asked why they were not prosecuted. The chairman also expressed concern at the reporting of other cases, notably that of a youth who had discharged a blank pistol at the Queen, and raised the question of whether the publicity had exceeded permissible limits. The Attorney General replied that 'it was not in the public interest that a very large number of editors and others should be paraded in front of the Divisional Court'. In that context, he went on, it would have been absurd to prosecute a few editors for breaches of minor reporting restrictions. In relation to the other cases reported by the council chairman, the Attorney General replied that he had received no complaint on behalf of the defence. 'It seems inevitable that there should be extensive reporting of an apparent attack upon the Queen, witnessed by large numbers of people. I am not aware that the publicity included material which would be likely to prejudice a fair trial.'[32]

The council, in its report 'Press Conduct in the Sutcliffe Case', was somewhat critical of the Attorney General's tolerant attitude. Yet the Contempt Act, for all its faults, was at least designed to establish two vital freedoms of which the media had taken advantage, namely the right to report events of public interest, so long as the risk of *serious* prejudice to a trial was not *substantial,* and the right to have any possibility of criminal prosecutions decided by the Attorney General, applying broad considerations of public interest. It is ironic that a council committed to preserving freedom and upholding the right of the press to provide information of public interest and importance should seem to be in favour of the criminal prosecution of newspaper editors for providing just such information. The chairman's letter may well have encouraged the Attorney General to launch contempt prosecutions against five newspapers over their reporting of the arrest of Michael Fagan, the intruder in the Royal bedroom. In this instance it fell to the judges, rather than the council or the Attorney General, to tilt the public-interest balance in favour of the press. Apart from a 'lamentable example of journalistic invention' in the *Sunday Times,* the press was exonerated from the allegation that its reporting seriously prejudiced Fagan's right to a fair trial.[33]

Nevertheless, the council seems determined that its rulings should muzzle reports of court cases much further than either the law or the public interest requires. Its Sutcliffe report concluded that 'virtually nothing ought to have been published of what was said, or was apparent from the atmosphere, at the main West Yorkshire police press conference'.[34] Notwithstanding that the conference was shown on television the night before newspaper reports appeared, it ruled that the press should merely have reported that a man had been detained and would appear in court on a serious charge. In an equally indefensible ruling in

1983, it held that a Scottish newspaper acted 'improperly' by revealing that a man against whom rape charges had been dropped by the Crown had been previously jailed for attempted rape.[35] The man was not named, the report was true, and the victim, a teacher, had brought her ordeal into the open by complaining to the Lord Advocate. The public interest was served by informed criticism of prosecution policy, yet the council ruled that it was wrong to publish the information on which the criticism was based. Here again, the council is insisting upon a standard more onerous than the law requires, and is undermining, instead of preserving, an established freedom of the press to provide information about matters of public interest. Rulings of this restrictive sort will continue to come from a council which perceives itself as balancing press freedom in scales which give other interests equal weight. This is understandable, indeed unexceptionable, for a body which sets up as an independent judge between public and press. But who then will champion the press against the Press Council?

Conclusion

Can the work of protecting press freedom safely be left to the many organizations which lay claim to concern? The NUJ, the Guild of British Newspaper Editors, the newspaper publishers' organizations, the Writers' Guild, the BBC, the Independent Television Companies' Association and the NCCL all share that interest. Yet the catalogue of defeats listed above is evidence enough of the inability of these disparate organizations to combat restrictions. It indicates a need for all media bodies to make common cause to defend their own freedoms, by establishing a new organization dedicated to watchfulness and to reforming the law. It is not necessary to advocate the libertarian position of the First Amendment in the USA ('Congress shall make no law abridging freedom of the Press'): Article 10 of the European Convention of Human Rights, which provides that there should be no infringement of freedom of expression unless it is *strictly necessary* to preserve overriding public interests, is a sufficient objective.[36] Nonetheless, this ideal is so far removed from the present law that it can only be secured by a broad-based lobbying effort on behalf of all media interests.

The Press Council *could*, under its present constitution, work to bring this about, either by itself, or in conjunction with other organizations. To shoulder the burden itself, to live up to its first objective, would require a massive commitment of time, money and resources. Media law is growing apace, and the council would have to set up a special section to comb impending legislation and court decisions, to publicize problems, support test cases and lobby for reform. This burden could of course be shared with other media interests: for example, the Independent Television Companies' Association was active and to some extent effective in combating the worst excesses of the Contempt of Court Bill. Were the Press Council to play a prominent part in such a movement, however, it might compromise, in the public mind, its position as an independent complaints tribunal. That position is, of course, already compromised by its first objective.

The British press does need a powerful champion against all the legal restrictions on investigative reporting. It requires an organization composed of eminent practitioners and distinguished sympathizers, funded and supported by groups representing workers, executives and owners of all printed and visual media, regularly publishing authoritative handbooks, guidelines and reform proposals aimed at enlarging the rights of journalists and broadcasters. The council cannot carry out this work, not just through lack of resources, but because to do so with the necessary commitment would undermine its function as an impartial adjudicator of public complaints.

6

Press Monopolies

The fifth object of the Press Council is: 'To report publicly on developments that may tend towards greater concentration or monopoly in the Press (including changes in ownership, control and growth of Press undertakings) and to publish statistical information relating thereto.' The original impetus for this objective came from the first Royal Commission on the Press. It identified the danger of monopolistic tendencies in the following terms:

> The monopolist, by its selection of the news and the manner in which it reports it, and by its commentary on public affairs, is in a position to determine what people shall read about the events and issues of the day, and to exert a strong influence on their opinions. Even if this position is not consciously abused, a paper without competitors may fall below the standards of accuracy and efficiency which competition enforces.[1]

One appropriate vehicle for combating undue concentration of ownership would, the first Royal Commission ventured, be the new Monopolies Commission, which had been established in 1948 to investigate whether certain restrictive practices operated against the public interest. The question of the stage at which a newspaper chain might become so large as to endanger the public interest could not be decided by any simple test: much would depend on the integration of the chain (particularly on the editorial side) and on the geographical concentration of its newspapers.[2] The Royal Commission did not recommend that its 'General Council of the Press' should make this decision: rather it should study and report on developments which might tend to greater concentration or monopoly, in order that parliament and the public could be alerted to the danger.[3]

Public Reporting

The Press Council's first Annual Report, published in 1954, managed to find space enough for only three paragraphs about changes in ownership. Significantly, that first report touched on the purchase of the *Scotsman* by a Canadian named Roy Thomson. The *Nottingham Journal*, it was also recorded, had been bought by T. Baily Forman Ltd, and promptly merged with that company's own paper, the *Nottingham Guardian*. Nottingham proved to be archetypal. There were four newspapers in that city when the Press Council began its work. There is now one, which is owned by T. Baily Forman.

Surprisingly, there were no developments worthy of note in the 1955 report, though a year later the council did record some changes, with a laconic comment that 'a number of provincial newspapers ceased publication and in every case this was attributed to rising costs of labour and newsprint'. The first serious review came in 1957, prompted perhaps by a parliamentary debate. Mr L.J. Cadbury, of the *News Chronicle* group, was quoted as saying that provincial newspapers were being eliminated at an alarming rate. Indeed they were. Fifteen titles died in that year alone, bringing the toll to fifty-five in six years. The Press Council was unruffled; it remarked, apropos the cost of newsprint, that newspapermen feared that more newspapers would be forced out of existence. The next two years brought nothing, apparently, deserving even a mention in the Annual Reports. Papers were bought and sold, titles died, choice diminished, all without public report or analysis from the council.

By 1959 Sir Linton Andrews had been succeeded as chairman of the council by George Murray – a change which had no discernible effect on the council's work. Those 'developments . . . that may tend towards greater concentration or monopoly' were persistently ignored. The 1960 report, for example, devoted a page and a half to newspaper changes, with fulsome welcomes for the *New Daily* (which died within a few weeks), the *Jerusalem Times* ('the only English-language daily paper in Jordan'), the *London-American*, the *National Christian News* and the *Anglican World*. Meanwhile, ten other titles had died without hope of resurrection.[4] In 1961, five major newspapers closed, despite the fact that their combined circulation was more than six million copies. The Press Council's analysis went no further than a statement that 1961 was 'the blackest year in the history of Fleet

Street'.[5] There was no attempt at any review of long-term developments in the industry: the Annual Reports throughout the early sixties simply recorded losses and closures, with a lame comment such as: 'This trend, attributed to the pressure of economic circumstances, is deplored, because newspapers play a vital role in the life of the community.'[6]

The second Royal Commission, chaired by Lord Shawcross and reporting in 1962, was scathing about the council's failure to study the economic and social factors which had produced concentrations of ownership. It commented:

> The Council's study of the economic problems facing the Press appears to have been mainly confined to the preparation of a bald factual account of some of the changes in the number and ownership of newspapers which have occurred in each year. Full advantage has certainly not been taken of the existence of a body representing the Press as a whole to enlarge public knowledge of the problems which the Press have to face. In evidence before us the representatives of the Council stated that the extent to which they could deal with economic matters was limited by their lack of power to call for information and that the scale of their financial resources limited the extent of the activities they could undertake. It must be pointed out that these limitations are entirely the result of the policies pursued by the Council's constituent bodies. We were not told that the Council had ever pressed for a substantial increase in its funds. . . . It is sufficient for present purposes to say that the Council as now constituted has not been and is not able to make any significant contribution to the solution of the broad problems which we are called upon to consider.[7]

The Shawcross Commission said that, had the council done its work properly, by enlarging public knowledge of developments tending towards monopoly, some of the more adverse consequences of these developments might have been averted. For the future, it recommended that the council should undertake the following functions:

- Scrutinise changes in the ownership, control and growth of Press undertakings (including periodical undertakings so far as they are relevant to the public interest), and give wide publicity to authoritative information on these matters in annual reports or by special report if the need arose.

• Keep up to date and publish statistical information relevant to ownership concentrations in the Press.[8]

Twenty years after Shawcross, the council still does not fulfil either of these functions. It does publish, at the back of each Annual Report, tables detailing press holdings and circulation for that year. But since these reports are published three to four years after the year in question, the details of press holdings are always out of date. The council has never published a special report, despite occasions which might seem to have called for one (e.g. when *The Times*, the *Sunday Times* and the *Observer* were sold in early 1981). Its annual reports fail to give 'wide publicity to authoritative information' on monopolistic developments. The only concession in this respect is a chapter containing a journalistic account, generally of one newspaper or publishing house each year. This chapter is always prefaced with the following statement:

> Conforming with the principles enunciated by the second Royal Commission on the Press, the Council offers, without comment, an independent examination of the structure of some of Britain's leading newspaper organisations.

These unattributed 'independent examinations' do not, in fact, conform with the principles enunciated by the second Royal Commission. They generally take the form of an historical examination of only one particular publishing organization or newspaper. They do not conform with the Shawcross principle, which required *scrutiny* of 'changes in the ownership, control and growth of Press undertakings'. They are offered, moreover, 'without comment': the whole point of the Shawcross principle was that they should be offered with authoritative and, where necessary, critical comment. The chapter has failed to appear in the council's most recent report, for the year of 1979, which was published in November 1982. With or without the chapter, it remains fair to say that the council's Annual Reports are bereft of analysis and criticism of monopolistic tendencies in the British press.

Enter the Monopolies Commission

The principal recommendation of the second Royal Commission was for new legislation to enable press amalgamations and mergers to be scrutinized by an independent body. This tribunal would grant consent to a transaction only if it were shown to serve the public interest in the accurate presentation of news and the free expression of opinion. Transactions to which the statute would apply (i.e. those which involved the sale of a newspaper with a circulation above 300,000 copies) would be presumed to be contrary to the public interest unless the applicants could prove that freedom and variety of opinion were not likely to be reduced by the transaction. The commission recommended the establishment of a 'Press Amalgamations Court' empowered to be final arbiter; the Monopolies Commission, it pointed out, had no power other than to make a report to a government minister. The dangers of a narrow and sectional press were too great to be left to party political considerations; the decision to approve a newspaper sale 'should be kept entirely free of Government responsibility or political association'.[9]

The wisdom of this approach was borne out for many in 1981, when a Conservative government refused even to submit the takeover of Times Newspapers by the Australian businessman, Rupert Murdoch, to the Monopolies Commission. However, it was a Labour government, in 1965, which emasculated the Shawcross proposal. Instead of setting up an Amalgamations Court, it decided to give additional powers to the Board of Trade (subsequently, to the Secretary of State for Trade) to refer proposed newspaper mergers to the Monopolies Commission. The procedure is now set out in Sections 57–61 of the Fair Trading Act. The minister is, in certain circumstances, required to refer newspaper sales or mergers to the Monopolies Commission. The commission must report back to the minister, within three months, on 'whether the transfer in question may be expected to operate against the public interest, taking into account all matters which appear in the circumstances to be relevant and, in particular, the need for accurate presentation of news and free expression of opinion'.[10] Transfers of newspapers to proprietors whose existing press interests (together with the acquired newspaper) have a circulation in excess of 500,000 copies a day are unlawful without the consent of the Secretary of State, unless the newspaper acquired is 'not economic as a going concern'.

In 1965, when these reforms were put to parliament, the Press Council protested vigorously. It expostulated that this measure, although a watered-down attempt to further an objective of the council's own constitution, was an exercise in government control which threatened press freedom, a right for which 'the common people had fought and died'.[11] Those common people might have evinced posthumous surprise that the right, in the council's view, apparently included the power to close and dispose of a mass-circulation newspaper at will. One answer to the objection that such legislation interferes with press freedom was forcefully given by Mr Justice Douglas, when American newspapers claimed that their First Amendment rights were threatened by the stringent anti-monopoly provisions of the Sherman Act:

It would be strange indeed if the grave concern for freedom of the press which prompted adoption of the First Amendment should be read as a command that the government was without power to protect that freedom. That Amendment rests on the assumption that the widest possible dissemination of information from diverse and antagonistic sources is essential to the welfare of the public, and that a free press is a condition of a free society. Surely a command that the government itself shall not impede the free flow of ideas does not afford non-governmental combinations a refuge if they impose restraints upon that constitutionally guaranteed freedom. Freedom to publish means freedom for all and not for some. Freedom to publish is guaranteed by the Constitution but freedom to combine to keep others from publishing is not. Freedom of the press from governmental interference under the First Amendment does not sanction repression of that freedom by private interests. The First Amendment affords not the slightest support for the contention that a combination to restrain trade in news and views has any constitutional immunity.[12]

The council's shortsighted opposition to the idea of a statutory reference to the Monopolies Commission was a regrettable, and regretted, incident in its history. Three years later, after the first two referrals had been heard by the commission, the council changed its tune. It was forced 'to support the view that the new legislation . . . is acting as a curb on the trend towards Press takeovers'.[13]

That remains the council's revised view. But, as the following will demonstrate, it is doubtful whether the present statutory provisions for press-merger references are in fact adequate to combat unhealthy concentrations of newspaper ownership.

The Press Council and the Monopolies Commission

The Monopolies Commission could scarcely have been given a more important test case than the 1966 application to sell *The Times* to the Thomson Organization. In spite of being the owner of two television companies, thirty-three newspapers (including the *Sunday Times*), sixty-two magazines and numerous other interests in publishing, Lord Thomson's purchase of *The Times* from Lord Astor met with the commission's approval. Dealing with the question of concentration of ownership, the commission admitted in its report to parliament that Thomson's takeover of *The Times* 'would be a continuation of the movement towards concentration in the ownership of the press, which must ultimately tend to stifle the expression of variety of opinion'. The report went on, however, to say that the commission did 'not consider that the proposed transfer would lead to an *undue* concentration of newspaper power'. It was equally tolerant when laying down the conditions which were to be attached to any transfer of ownership of *The Times*. Although recognizing that a proposal to put four 'national figures' on the main board of Times Newspapers Ltd would be merely 'window dressing' – 'no more than a declaration of good intent by the Thomson Organization designed to reassure the public' – the commission lamely agreed to the proposal on the grounds that it could devise nothing better. [14]

The Press Council's attitude and role in this crucial test of the monopolies legislation in relation to newspapers is unclear. The council is listed among those organizations which gave evidence to the commission, and tribute for help with statistical information is paid to the council in the final report, but there is no suggestion that it was hostile to the takeover of Britain's most prestigious newspaper by a Canadian press baron. The council's historian, H. Phillip Levy, simply records that 'Lord Devlin gave evidence to the Monopolies Commission on behalf of the Press Council.' [15] The 1967 report of the Press Council's work contains a bland account of the Thomson takeover at Printing House Square and of the Monopolies Commission investigation. Admitting that there was 'public concern about the continued trend towards greater concentration or monopoly in the Press', the report is nonetheless silent as to the council's own view on the takeover, other than noting that the council was itself charged with the duty of reporting on anything which might lead to concentration of ownership.

By the late 1960s and early 1970s, the Press Council was paying attention to matters such as privacy, contempt, secrecy and defamation. But on takeovers, monopolies, closures and suchlike the council reverted to silence. Others were raising their voices and their concern, however. Lord Pearce, who succeeded Lord Devlin as chairman, conceded in his last report (1973) that there was 'unease' at the political and economic hazards facing newspapers and that 'any disappearance of a newspaper must occasion worry'.[16] The Monopolies Commission was much more forthright. Despite giving its approval to the takeover of another eighteen newspapers by the Westminster Press group, the commission called for a special government enquiry into concentration of ownership.[17]

Before giving its approval to the Westminster Press takeover, the Monopolies Commission invited the Press Council to submit its views. The response was that '. . . whereas Westminster Press were a reliable company and had a good record', the council 'found it impossible to say that it was in the public interest that a further concentration of weekly newspapers in that area in one set of hands should be allowed'.[18] This conclusion fell short of stating that the takeover was *against* the public interest – the test applied by the Monopolies Commission for withholding consent. In 1974 the Press Council was asked by the commission for its views on the takeover of five more titles by Associated Newspapers. The council responded by saying that it 'had not sufficient information on which to base a view as to whether the transfer was in the public interest'.[19]

In 1981 Times newspapers was sold to Rupert Murdoch, thereby concentrating a large amount of national newspaper power in one controversial pair of hands. Ownership of the *Sun* and *The Times* gave Murdoch a 30% share of daily newspaper readership, while the *Sunday Times* and the *News of the World* added up to a 36% share of Sunday readership. The ethical record of Murdoch's British papers was questionable, and his reputation in Australia and America for interfering with editorial independence and exploiting his papers for political purposes raised serious doubts about whether the takeover could serve the public interest. Some enquiry was called for, and it might have encompassed Murdoch's attitude towards Press Councils. When the Australian Press Council, which is chaired by a High Court judge, had censured one of his newspapers for irresponsible reportage of an election campaign, Murdoch's response was simply to withdraw all suport from the council, and decline to recognize its adjudications. All these matters could and should have been investigated by the Monopolies Commission, on a reference from the Secretary of State for Trade, John Biffen.

However, the legislation requiring referral allows an exemption if the minister is satisfied that the newspaper to be purchased is 'not economic as a going concern' – an accurate description of *The Times*, but not of the *Sunday Times*. The journalists of the *Sunday Times* were advised by Queen's Counsel that they had a good case in law for obliging the minister to refer the sale to the commission, and they commenced to take the minister to court. Two days before the case was to be heard they dropped it – partly through concern at the risk of legal costs should it be fought through all appellate stages. The Press Council did not pick up the dropped baton by bringing, or offering to support, an action to oblige the gc /ernment to make a referral. The minister approved the transfer subject tc certain conditions involving independent directors.

The minister's approval of the takeover was announced in the House of Commons in the course of a debate on the subject during the afternoon of 27 January 1981. It was clear from the terms of the announcement that the minister had made up his mind at an earlier stage. The Press Council's behaviour was curious in the extreme. It said nothing until 27 January, i.e. until after the minister had made the decision. At some stage on that day it issued a short press release calling for the takeover to be referred to the Monopolies Commission. This press release was not published in time for the three-hour debate in parliament held that afternoon; certainly it was not mentioned by any speaker. In other words, the council's timing of its expression of opinion was such as to render its opinions irrelevant both to the decision itself and to the parliamentary debate over that decision. It may pay lip-service to its constitutional duty to warn against monopolies, but on this most important occasion it did not move its lips in time for any warning to be heeded.

The refusal by the government to refer the takeover of Times Newspapers to the Monopolies Commission illustrates the inadequacy of the referral procedure embodied in the Fair Trading Act as a method of scrutinizing concentrations of ownership. Rupert Murdoch had threatened to withdraw from the transaction if a Monopolies Commission referral were made, and the purchase had been engineered to a time-table which could not accommodate the time which a proper investigation would take. The Press Council, in its press release, 'stressed the need for a very speedy report by the Commission, which would take into account the utmost urgency surrounding the future of the papers'. [20] This response by the council went out of its way to lend credence to the 'urgency' of the situation – a claim which had been used by the parties to the transaction to escape a referral, which could only be avoided if the minister was satisfied, not only as to the economic plight of the newspapers, but also that 'the case is one of urgency'. [21] Thus, although the council belatedly called for an enquiry, the terms of its appeal could only play into the hands of those who wished to justify the minister's decision to avoid one. The council later claimed to be 'seized of the difficulties posed by the time-table set for transfer by the parties', without any criticism of parties who deliberately chose a time-table which made no allowance for a Monopolies Commission enquiry. [22] It is interesting to note that the council press release added: 'The Press Council would be prepared to help by providing its views forthwith to the commission.' It did not provide any views to the public, nor to parliament at the time when the desirability of a Monopolies Commission referral was being debated. It will be necessary to wait until 1984 (when the council's Annual Report for 1981 may be published) to see what those views might have been – if the council then thinks fit to disclose them.

In March 1981, a few weeks after *The Times* takeover, Atlantic Richfield, the US oil company which had owned the *Observer* since 1976, announced that it was selling the paper to Mr 'Tiny' Rowlands of Lonrho. Once again, efforts were made by the parties to avoid any detailed examination of the nature of the takeover. Although its tendency to concentrate ownership was much less dramatic than Rupert Murdoch's acquisition of Times Newspapers, Mr Biffen this time agreed to refer the matter to the Monopolies Commission.

The Press Council was among the bodies which gave evidence to the ensuing enquiry. It asserted (with scant historical justification) that it was the council's 'consistent view' that further concentration of ownership of control of newspapers was undesirable. The council went on to say that it did *not* believe 'that the proposed transfer would in itself lead to any concentration of ownership which would give rise to any significant social problems or dangers'. It was, therefore, in favour of the takeover. The council did express concern, however, about the possible effect 'on the presentation of news and free expression of opinion' because of Lonrho's area of operation and style of management. More diffidently, it entered reservations about the manner in which the takeover had been attempted and said it was 'difficult to have confidence in the assertions made by the parties to the transfer, concerning such matters as the continuing independence of the newspaper'.[23]

These concerns led it to suggest to the Monopolies Commission that the transfer should only be allowed 'subject to very strict conditions'. These conditions were that independent directors or trustees be appointed, to whom any dispute between the editor and the owners should be referred. The council further suggested that the approval of the independent directors or trustees should be required for the appointment or dismissal of the editor. The council does not appear to have considered the nub of the problem, namely, the difficulty of achieving public confidence in 'independent directors' who owed their appointment to the proprietor. The idea of independent directors had, of course, been described as 'window dressing' by the commission at the time it was first mooted. The 1966 Monopolies Commission report into the Thomson takeover of *The Times* had rejected a suggestion that the 'national directors' should have a veto over the dismissal of the editor. The commission's report pointed out that 'no such provision could be made permanently effective against a proprietor owning 85% of the company'. It went on: 'Proprietors may choose to give their editors a free hand . . . but this does not alter the fact that newspapers remain the property of their proprietors, who have the right to decide what form this property should take.'[24]

The Monopolies Commission recommended that the transfer be allowed provided, amongst other things, that 'independent directors' were appointed by Lonrho. It accepted that

. . . the proposed transfer involving a major provincial publisher acquiring a national title does represent yet another move in the continuing growth of concentration of ownership of provincial and national newspapers, *which was seriously increased by the recent acquisition of* The Times *and* Sunday Times *by companies controlled by Mr Rupert Murdoch.*[25]

Conclusion

Over the last thirty years the process of concentration of newspaper ownership in Britain has developed alarmingly. More than

70% of all national daily newspapers are now published by four multi-national companies; more than 80% of national Sunday newspapers are published by the same four companies; and in the provinces large numbers of local papers are controlled by four conglomerates: Thomson Regional Newspapers, Associated Newspapers (which also publishes the *Daily Mail*), Westminster Press (linked to the *Financial Times* and *Economist*) and Reed International (owners of Mirror Group Newspapers). Britain now has one of the most concentrated newspaper ownership arrangements in the western world. Yet the Press Council has uttered few words of warning, let alone condemnation.

It is easy to find reasons for this failure. With hindsight, the council's mistake has been to approach every change of ownership as if it were a one-off event, rather than part of a wider pattern. It has not sought to analyse the overall trend towards concentration of ownership. Its lack of resources provides an explanation, but not an excuse; it could, as the second Royal Commission pointed out, request further funds from its backers to enable it to fulfil this constitutional objective. These backers, of course, are the very ownerships which have tended to concentrate; a Press Council vigilant against takeovers would have to bite some of the hands that feed it. There is no reason why a truly independent Press Council should not oppose the commercial aspirations of its backers; it is simply a fact that its opposition to takeovers has always been muted.

There must be some effective and independent safeguard for the public good against the development of press monopolies, and no amount of restructuring could enable the Press Council to fulfil that function. The Shawcross proposal for a Press Amalgamations Court free from party political considerations remains the most satisfactory model, but the improbability of any government relinquishing its right to make a final decision renders the Amalgamations Court a politically unrealistic proposition. There remains only the Monopolies Commission which has, under the present terms of the Fair Trading Act, no power beyond that of presenting a report to the appropriate minister. If the Monopolies Commission is properly to oversee monopolistic tendencies in the press, a number of amendments to the Fair Trading Act would be required:

• At present, the law allows the Secretary of State to give unconditional consent to a transfer without reference to the Monopolies Commission if satisfied that the newspaper to be sold is 'not economic as a going concern'.[26] The very fact that the government could decide, in 1981, that the *Sunday Times* fell into this category, on the basis of highly questionable projections of future income supplied by parties to the sale who were eager to avoid a referral, shows how easily the requirements may be sidestepped. Where the intention is to keep the newspaper alive as a separate publication (a fact which would normally indicate that it was a viable economic proposition) the minister may consent if 'the case is one of urgency'.[27] Again, in the *Sunday Times* case, that urgency was dictated by the time-table devised by the parties to the transaction. In cases where the intention is to close the newspaper, or to absorb it under a rival title, the minister has no alternative but to give unconditional consent to the sale.[28] Such transactions can sometimes be avoided by arrangements which still give the selling proprietor a reasonable recompense.

If the Monopolies Commission is to have effective control over concentrations of ownership in the newspaper industry, all those loopholes in the Fair Trading Act will need to be closed. Whether the paper is 'economic as a going concern' would then be one of the factors the commission could take into account in deciding whether to recommend the transfer, after its own independent assessment of the viability of the newspaper's future and after considering any alternative offers which would preserve publication or avoid further concentration of ownership.

● The public-interest test which the Monopolies Commission has applied in its nine reports on newspaper transfers since 1965 is unsatisfactory. Under the Fair Trading Act it is required to report on 'whether the transfer in question may be expected to operate against the public interest'.[29] The burden of proving this speculation falls upon opponents of the transfer. As the third Royal Commission pointed out: 'In individual cases it is almost impossible to establish this to the Commission's satisfaction and in none of the cases so far referred has it been established.'[30] That Royal Commission recommended that the Monopolies Commission should reverse its onus of proof: it should withhold approval unless positively satisfied that the merger would *not* operate against the public interest. This is the test applied in other restrictive-trade practices legislation and the Royal Commission believed it would 'provide a more satisfactory basis for judgement by the Commission'.

● One important aspect in a newspaper transfer is, as all Royal Commissions have recognized, the danger of creating an imbalance in the political affiliations of the press. Newspapers have, as the Press Council has continually held, a right to be politically partisan; it must be against the public interest if press outlets in a particular area, or in the nation as a whole, come, as a result of monopolistic tendencies, to favour overwhelmingly one particular side of the political spectrum. However, when this question was raised by some objectors to the Lonrho takeover of the *Observer* (i.e. the danger that a politically neutral newspaper might, by the decision of its new proprietor, join the ranks of papers supporting the Conservative Party) the commission declared it inadmissible. 'It would be a serious development of our role for us to take such a point into account' was its reason for refusing to examine the proposed proprietor's political plans for the newspaper.[31] While the commission's reluctance to examine proprietorial politics is understandable, the Fair Trading Act requires it to take into account 'all matters which appear in the circumstances to be relevant' to the question of whether the transfer would operate against the public interest. This does not call for an evaluation of the merits of political policies, but an assessment of the consequences of the transaction on the availability to the public of a reasonable variety of editorial opinion. It is a serious mistake for the Monopolies Commission to interpret the Act so as to disallow consideration of this important dimension.

● In cases of newspaper merger referrals, the Monopolies Commission must report within three months, and must include in that report 'a survey of the general position' with respect to the transfer, 'and of developments which have led to that position'.[32] It may recommend that the government attach conditions to the transfer which would minimize dangers to the public interest. These statutory duties call for considerable investigation and knowledge of the industry, and up to five additional members may be appointed by the government to assist the commission in such referrals.[33] However, this power of ad hoc appointment is no substitute for the commission being placed in a position to judge, from its own monitoring work, what the impact of a particular sale is likely to be. This could be achieved if the Monopolies Commission were given a permanent responsibility to monitor, and from time to time to report publicly on, developments which tend towards greater concentration of press holdings. Such developments are of great consequence to a democracy, as three Royal Commissions have painstakingly established. The significance of press combines is already recognized, albeit imperfectly, in the special newspaper provisions of the Fair Trading Act. A standing referral, together with the amendments to the Act recommended above, would allow these developments to be watched and, where they conflict with the public interest, to be contained by an authoritative organization entirely independent of the media.

These reforms in the Monopolies Commission would not mean that the Press Council need abandon its constitutional concern with press monopolies, but rather that this concern should take a different form. The council's basic function is to adjudicate disputes between newspapers and the public, and to encourage the development of high ethical standards. In reporting to the Monopolies Commission on whether a particular takeover might work against the public interest, it should consider the ethical record of the bidding group, and should have no hesitation in opposing further acquisitions by a proprietor whose existing papers had flouted the council's standards and failed to comply with its adjudications. This would provide it with a long-term deterrent – a sanction which it has hitherto failed to use. An important aspect in any press takeover would be the ethical performance of the group which wished to enlarge its holdings – and that group would be called upon to justify, on peril of being declared unfit for further ownership, any refusal to cooperate with the council's work. The council should not hesitate, in its Annual Reports, to comment on the performance in this respect of every newspaper proprietor, leaving no doubt in the public mind as to which organizations are collectively and consistently falling below standard. The consequences of a consistently low rating – namely, the failure to win approval for further media acquisitions – would provide publishers with an economic incentive to abide by the council's rulings. Such an incentive is at present sorely lacking.

7
Reform of the Press Council

Oh dear, oh dear. I have great admiration for the Press
Council, and strongly believe one should always keep a
hold of nurse, for fear of finding something worse.
Auberon Waugh, 'Wine and the Press Council'[1]

The performance of the Press Council has been measured in this
book against the yardsticks provided by its own constitutional
objectives. In each respect – the adjudication of public
complaints, the maintenance of ethical standards, the defence of
press freedom and the combating of monopolistic tendencies –
the evidence has dictated the conclusion that the council does not
satisfactorily achieve these objectives. Some of its failures stem
from deficiencies which could be redressed within its present
structure, and others call for entirely new arrangements. But,
whatever the temptation to scrap a defective organization and
start afresh, there must be certain concessions to existing systems
and political realities. The Press Council works against the background of a legal system which believes in freedom of expression
as long as it does not express too much. With an understandable
fear of regulation by the heavy hand of statute law, the dominant
purpose of the council has been to safeguard the industry against
the encroachment of press law. But laws may work *for* the press,
as well as against it. If, say, a Freedom of Information Act and
libel-law reform were offered to the media, in exchange for its
acceptance of a legal right to privacy and a right of reply, the
bargain would be overwhelmingly in the interests of both public
and press. But since law reform tends not to come in such
convenient packages, a more piecemeal process must be
examined.

Drawing upon the evidence presented earlier in the book, this chapter will begin by urging that the Press Council discard those functions it has proved least capable of performing. That will leave such tasks as the adjudication of public complaints and the setting of ethical standards. These areas raise a major problem – the correction of factual mis-statements – which neither a 'representative' Press Council nor its alternative, the law of libel, can satisfactorily address. It will be suggested that both Press Council and libel law should be replaced in these cases by a Press Ombudsman, created by statute to afford a new remedy which is neither protracted nor expensive, and which carries, as its only threat to press freedom, a deterrent to the freedom to fabricate news. The Press Council would survive as a body shaped, much more precisely and powerfully than at present, to monitor and to censure deviations from properly formulated ethical standards. Were this sort of order to be established, the press and the media generally would be in better shape to demand reforms in laws which unnecessarily shackle investigative reporting.

Press Freedom For the reasons set out in Chapter 5, the objective of protecting press freedom has proved incompatible with the council's primary function of complaints adjudication. The objective is of great importance, but it compromises the council's posture as an impartial and independent adjudicator of public complaints, and has inevitably been subordinated in recent years to this dominant purpose. Moreover, it is not an objective confined to the sectional interest of newspapers: it equally affects television, film and book publishing. It is truly a media issue, and defence against legal encroachments requires the establishment of an expert organization representative of all sections of the media. There has been an increasing tendency for legislation and case-law to cut back established freedom, and media interests have not lobbied very effectively against these tendencies. In the days of Lords Devlin and Pearce, the Press Council was able authoritatively to defend the interests of the press; those days cannot return, because of the dominance and importance of its complaints function. Until a broadly based 'media guard' organization is established, the press will continue to suffer from the absence of a vigilant spokesman.

Concentration of ownership Chapter 6 described the council's poor record in combating concentration of ownership in the newspaper industry. This task should and could be performed by the Monopolies Commission, assuming it were given a standing reference on the subject and necessary amendments were made to the Fair Trading Act. There remains one important role for a reformed Press Council in newspaper takeovers, namely, to advise the Monopolies Commission on the record of the bidding group in complying with adjudications and upholding Press Council standards. This would provide the council with a valuable long-term economic sanction, and be an added incentive for proprietors to make sure that their newspapers complied with its rulings. It would be desirable for the council to add a section to its Annual Report in which it assessed the ethical performance of each newspaper group – an assessment based both on the evidence culled from individual adjudications, and on the results of a new monitoring system.

Complaints and standards The heart of the Press Council's work – its adjudication of complaints and its maintenance of press standards – is described in Chapters 3 and 4. Attention is drawn to the council's capacity for delay at every stage, the obstacles placed in the path of complainants, its lack of powers to ensure compliance with its rulings, and its failure to develop coherent standards, amongst other debilitating features of its operations. The evidence makes a powerful case for reform, if not for outright replacement, of the council by a new body empowered by law to enforce its rulings.

Demands for a statutory Press Council have come from many quarters. The Institute of Journalists (IOJ), for example, proposed to the third Royal Commission that legislation be introduced to provide for a 'register of journalists', like the register of doctors maintained by the General Medical Council. Journalists would be suspended, or struck off entirely, for 'unprofessional behaviour'.[2] The draconian sanctions advocated by the IOJ are reflected in many other proposals for statutory discipline of the press, made from all parts of the political spectrum.

The arguments of principle against any system for 'licensing' either journalists or newspapers are set out in Chapter 4. The 'right to write' is fundamental to freedom of expression. Because it is a right, rather than a privilege, it cannot be withdrawn. Unethical exercises of the right should not silence a journalist or an editor 'for a period or indefinitely' as proposed by the IOJ. Those who exercise a right available to all may be made to suffer for irresponsible conduct, but they must at least be allowed to shriek at their punishment. That said, however, what should be the appropriate response to flagrant breaches of ethical standards: to factual inaccuracies, distortion, unfair comment, fabrication of news, invasion of privacy, cheque-book journalism and the like?

There is a crucial distinction to be made between mis-statements of fact and other forms of press irresponsibility. Facts should be sacred, and it is a proper function of the law to provide a speedy method of correction and redress in the case of demonstrable mistakes. A body as cumbersome as the existing Press Council, composed of a large and broadly representative group of press and public, may be appropriate for passing judgement on newspaper ethics. It is an entirely inappropriate vehicle for affording a remedy for factual mis-statements, which require immediate correction if their damage is to be minimized. The council is lacking in both powers and procedures to correct mistakes promptly and prominently, and no amount of reform will put it in a position to do so. But what of the present alternative to the Press Council – an action for defamation?

The law of libel The victim of damaging press inaccuracy who fails to obtain satisfaction from the editor by way of a correction or a published reply will be better advised to ignore the Press Council and instruct a lawyer. A solicitor will write a 'letter before action' to the newspaper, threatening a writ for libel unless a correction in terms drafted by, or acceptable to, the victim is immediately forthcoming. This will sometimes have the desired effect. If it does not, and the victim is reasonably wealthy, a writ for libel will be issued. Within a few weeks of the original error, the newspaper will be called upon to 'justify' its statement in its 'particulars of defence' – a legal document which must be filed with the court, setting out the facts which will be relied upon to show that the complained-of statement is true. If the newspaper's lawyers do not consider there is sufficient evidence to justify the original statement there will generally be a settlement at this point effected by an apology in open court (which may be published in other newspapers), a prominent correction and apology in the newspaper, and a payment to the plaintiff of legal costs and sometimes substantial damages. In rare cases – where the litigant is wealthy and the editor (and the proprietor) determined, the case may proceed to trial. The point to note is that, when a real and damaging error is made, the victim who is wealthy enough to retain a lawyer will often obtain a satisfactory settlement either immediately or within a reasonable time of the original publication. By comparison, the Press Council is a poor substitute and, because legal aid is not available for libel actions, it can be a poor person's only substitute.

● *Should legal aid be available for libel actions?* Defamation is the *only* branch of common law for which legal aid is unavailable. This stark inequity means that wealthy plaintiffs, and those who are backed by professional trade associations, enjoy privileged access to a powerful weapon of redress. And it means that newspapers may print the most deliberate or reckless lies about poor people, secure in the knowledge that the victim cannot afford the thousands of pounds cost of financing preliminary legal skirmishings, let alone the potentially vast legal fees of a contested trial. However, the extension of legal aid for libel is not a satisfactory solution to the problem of securing redress for factual mis-statements. For a start, there are many newspaper errors which the libel law cannot correct. And although it may work wonders in some deserving cases, it often works the same wonders in undeserving ones as well. There would be more 'gagging' writs, more gold-digging actions, more public-interest stories put on the spike because of the impossibility of proving them by admissible evidence, and more dilution of free speech. The case against libel law as the means of rectifying false statements may be summarized as follows:

● *Libel law does not rectify all false statements.* Libel law does not provide a remedy for all, or even most, factual mis-statements. It can only be activated when a false statement actually damages a reputation. An assertion is not defamatory simply because it is untrue – it must lower the victim in the eyes of right-thinking citizens. However irksome it may be to have inaccuracies published about one's life or behaviour – dates mis-stated, nonexistent meetings described, qualifications misattributed, and so on, there must be a 'sting' in the falsehood which reflects discredit in the eyes of society. To publish falsely, of an Irish priest, that he informed on members of the IRA is not defamatory. It may cause him to be executed by terrorists, but the law offers him no way of securing a correction: 'The very circumstances which will make a person be regarded with dis-favour by the criminal classes will raise his character in the estimation of right-thinking men. We can only regard the estimation in which a man is held by society generally.'[3] This aspect of the libel law is often forgotten. During the 'Right of

Reply' debate in Parliament, Sir Phillip Goodhart recalled how, at the height of a by-election shortly after the Suez crisis, the local newspaper reported him as saying that John Foster Dulles was a good friend of this country. 'I had in fact said the precise opposite. On the advice of Conservative Central Office I abandoned my campaign and went hot-foot to the leading libel advocate of the day. He, alas, said that no libel had taken place, although a great inaccuracy had occurred. There was no redress.'[4] In 1981, the Court of Appeal held that to say of a healthy person that he is 'very seriously ill and unlikely to recover' is not defamatory.[5]

● *Libel law discourages true statements about matters of public interest.* A libel is, in effect, a criticism of a person or corporation. The facts stated may well be true, but the newspaper carries, in law, the burden of *proving* they are true, by testimony which satisfies strict rules of evidence law. It follows that where the source for a story dies, or is out of the country, or has been promised confidentiality, it will be difficult for the newspaper to satisfy that legal burden. In America and in most Western European countries, newspapers are provided with a specific public-interest defence which allows them to escape damages if they show that they had reasonable grounds for believing statements published about important persons and organizations. This defence has no equivalent in British law, and there are a number of recorded cases where damages have been awarded for libellous statements subsequently proved true.

● *Libel law and procedure is much too complicated.* Libel law has been allowed to become hideously complex. One straight-forward case – involving a 'Police Five' warning on television about a confidence trickster whose alias was the same name as the plaintiff's – had consequences devastatingly described by Lord Diplock:

This is an ordinary simple case of libel. It took fifteen days to try: the summing-up lasted for a day: the jury returned thirteen special verdicts. The notice of appeal sets out seven separate grounds why the appeal should be allowed and ten more why a new trial should be granted, the latter being split up into over forty sub-grounds. The respondent's notice contained fifteen separate grounds. The costs must be enormous. Lawyers should be ashamed that they have allowed the law of defamation to have become bogged down in such a mass of technicalities that this should be possible.[6]

That case was heard in 1966, since when the 'mass of technicalities' has been piled much higher.

● *Libel cases can be protracted and expensive.* Libel actions launched by wealthy and determined plaintiffs are frighteningly expensive to combat. Even if successful, the defendant is unlikely to recoup all the costs. When the *Daily Mail* was sued by the head of the Unification Church in Britain over allegations that the 'Moonies' brainwashed converts and broke up families, the editor was warned by his lawyers that an adverse verdict might, with legal costs and damages, cost him £1 million. The case lasted a hundred days, required the attendance of many witnesses from abroad, and the defendant's legal costs alone amounted to some £400,000. The complexities of the pleadings and the pressure on court time can produce long delays in contested cases. Plaintiffs can issue a writ anytime within six years of the publication complained about, and several years invariably lapse between the issue of the writ and the trial of the action.

● *Libel damages are not only unprincipled but also unpredictable.* Damages for libel are notoriously unpredictable. Women who are raped receive about £2000 compensation from the Criminal Injuries Compensation Board. But when film star Telly Savalas sued over a gossip columnist's unjustified remarks about hangovers interfering with his work, he was awarded £34,000. The foreman of his jury wrote to *The Times*:

> . . . where a jury has to decide, as men and women of the world, 'how much', the degree of uncertainty is so great that a random answer, consistent only with a total lack of any sort of yardstick, can be expected. Their Lordships would do as well to use an Electronic Random Number Indicating Machine.[7]

Immediate cries went up for trial by judges alone. But judges have dispensed the same capricious largesse: they can lean to titled or establishment litigants, while juries are impressed by show-business plaintiffs and know (or think) that newspapers make large profits.

Each case which goes to trial is an elaborate gamble: how much should be paid into court, and when? A 'payment into court' is a tactical ploy, kept secret from the jury. If the defendant makes a payment, the plaintiff may seize it, plus his legal costs, and call quits. If the plaintiff presses on and wins, but is awarded no more in damages than the amount of the 'payment in', he must foot the entire legal bill incurred by both sides since the date of the payment. In one celebrated case in 1975, a colonel with a penchant for spanking unsuspecting women sued the *Sunday People* for exposing his activities; he was awarded a derisory halfpenny. But the newspaper was saddled with the legal costs of the trial, which it could have avoided by 'paying in' the lowest denomination coin of the realm before the trial began. The publishers of *Exodus* had greater foresight. When sued for libel by Dr Dering, an Auschwitz prison doctor criticized in the book, they 'paid in' the derisory sum of £2 before the trial. Dr Dering declined this contemptible compensation, and risked crippling legal costs on a trial which he hoped would win him heavy damages. The jury awarded him the libel raspberry – a halfpenny – so he was forced to pay for the whole action. In circumstances like these the Temple of Law becomes a casino.

Libel law is an expensive anachronism. The very idea that large sums of money must be awarded to compensate people for words which 'tend to lower them in the estimation of right-thinking members of society' smacks of an age when social and political life was lived in gentlemen's clubs, when escutcheons could be blotted and society scandals resolved by writs for slander. Libel damages call for a metaphysical evaluation of dignity, a compensation, in many cases, for loss of 'amour propre' which may be higher than the courts would award for the loss of an arm or a leg. The law should ensure both the speedy correction of false statements and the protection of the expression of honest opinion, but British law secures neither goal.

This is the point at which reform of the Press Council converges with reform of the libel law. Neither the present self-regulation system nor the present legal system satisfactorily provides for the speedy correction of factual inaccuracies. That object will not be achieved by giving the Press Council the power to do, by legal force, that which it does ineffectively. Nor will it be achieved by extending legal aid to enable greater advantage to be taken of a clumsy libel law. A new system must be devised to replace them both, maintaining the advantages of the Press Council (availability to all) and of the law (the power of enforcement) without the drawbacks of delay, technicality and hazard.

The Case for a Press Ombudsman

In 1967, parliament set up the office of Ombudsman (technically, the Parliamentary Commissioner for Administration) to investigate complaints by citizens who claimed to have suffered injustice at the hands of central or local government.[8] The impetus came from disenchantment with the methods of redress offered by the courts, which were limited and attended by delay and expense. The Ombudsman is empowered to examine claims of maladministration in the civil service – neglect, inattention, delay, incompetence, arbitrariness and the like – from a position of constitutional independence guaranteed by statute. The Ombudsman model originated in Scandinavia, and was first imported into the Westminster system via New Zealand.[9] It now works in many Commonwealth countries, rather more comprehensively than in Britain, to provide extra-legal redress for the citizen who has suffered at the hands of powerful agencies of the state. An Ombudsman for the Press exists in Sweden, in the form of a professional judge with his own staff, adjudicating complaints from the public and directing retractions or replies within a few days of the publication of inaccurate statements. In Britain, a Press Ombudsman would have many advantages for complainants and newspapers, if the office was constructed to replace both the libel law and the Press Council as a method of securing correction of mistakes by newspapers. It might work broadly in this way:

1 The Press Ombudsman would be created by statute as a full-time position with an independence, authority and salary equivalent to that of a High Court judge. The Ombudsman would have the right to appoint staff with suitable qualifications and investigative experience.

2 The office would call for a person respected for judgement and fact-finding ability. Someone in the Devlin or Scarman mould would be a desirable choice.

3 The Ombudsman would receive complaints against newspapers – i.e. against daily, Sunday, and provincial papers which routinely carry pages of news. Journals of opinion, trade or political magazines and the like would not be compelled to be part of the scheme, although they would be able to contract into it if they – or their libel insurers – wished to obtain its advantages.

4 The Ombudsman would be obliged to consider serious complaints alleging that newspapers had failed to correct statements containing errors of fact, or to publish replies to comments based upon factual mistakes.

5 The law of libel would cease to operate against newspapers, or any journals which agreed to be bound by the scheme, in respect of any article which could be made the subject of a complaint to the Ombudsman. In other words, the courts could not entertain libel actions about statements or comments which fell within the jurisdiction of the Ombudsman. The only exception to this rule would be in cases where the complainant wished to allege that a newspaper deliberately and maliciously published false information, knowing it to be false. This is the one area of libel law where heavy awards of damages *are* justifiable, and the issues would be more appropriately left to jury determination. In these rather rare cases, the plaintiff should be entitled, with legal aid if the strength of the case justifies it, to opt for libel law rather than the Ombudsman.

6 The Ombudsman's procedures would be designed to achieve a speedy resolution. Failing agreement between the parties, he would be under a duty to make a judgement within seven days of receiving the complaint, unless both sides agreed to allow additional time.

7 If the Ombudsman is satisfied that the newspaper published a factual error, he would be empowered to agree a correction (or failing agreement, to draft it himself) and to *order* the newspaper to carry it in a position or style which he considered appropriate to bring the mistake to the attention of the newspaper's readers. In cases where he is satisfied that a comment was unfair because it was based on a mistake or misunderstanding about the true or full facts, and that the appropriate form of redress is to publish the complainant's reply to the comment, he could order the newspaper to publish a reply of reasonable length.

8 The newspaper's only legal obligation under the above arrangement would be to carry the correction or reply, as directed. Its freedom of speech would be unimpaired. It would even be free to dissent from the Ombudsman's finding, although in that event it would lose its protection from libel action, and it would run the risk of losing a court battle against a plaintiff guaranteed legal aid.

9 The Ombudsman's office would be equipped to undertake rapid investigations, when necessary obtaining information additional to that provided by complainant and newspaper. All evidence supplied to the Ombudsman would enjoy the same privilege as if it had been given in a court of law. Newspapers could not be compelled to cooperate with the investigation, although failure to do so would carry an obvious risk of an adverse finding. The Ombudsman could reject trivial complaints without investigation, while unjustifiable allegations would be deterred by the prospect of the Ombudsman revealing the truth

rather more authoritatively than the original newspaper article. The Ombudsman would be debarred from revealing the identity of a newspaper source, if this were uncovered in the course of investigation, but the newspaper could, if it wished, reveal its source in strict confidence to the Ombudsman.

10 The Ombudsman's office would be autonomous, and subject only to the statutory duties set out in the Act which created it. One of those duties would be to publish an annual report, which would carry observations on the general performance of the press in achieving satisfactory levels of accuracy and fairness, and if necessary would identify and criticize any newspaper persistently publishing false or incomplete information.

11 The Ombudsman, as a creature of statute, would be subject to the customary methods of enforcing statutory powers and reviewing statutory duties. That is to say, in the unlikely event that a newspaper refused to accept a proper direction, the Ombudsman could obtain a court order obliging it to do so. Equally, the procedure would be open to review by the courts if the Ombudsman were shown to have acted in bad faith, or by an excess of power, or by breaching the rules of natural justice.

12 The Ombudsman's office would replace the Press Council as adjudicator of disputes over facts requiring immediate correction. However, there would be scope for productive liaison between the two bodies. If, in considering a complaint, the Ombudsman found that, in addition to issues of accuracy, it raised ethical questions which deserved consideration, he could refer it to the Press Council, with such information as his investigation had adduced.

13 The Ombudsman would have no power to fine or otherwise punish a newspaper or journalist, or to award the complainant damages for injury to reputation. However, he would be empowered to award *compensation,* for any actual and quantifiable loss suffered by the complainant as a result of the factual error, and for expenses properly incurred in bringing the complaint. The compensation fund would be provided by a levy on newspapers, with contributions fixed by reference to their circulation figures.

14 The Press Ombudsman would have as his main duty the correction of damaging factual inaccuracies in newspapers. As a judicial figure, independent of parliament and the courts, and with a sound knowledge of the press, he might fulfil another related and important role. Any Freedom of Information Act requires just such a figure to adjudicate disputes between the civil service and the media over whether documents demanded under the Act fall within a category exempted from disclosure (e.g. on grounds of national security). This task cannot readily fit into ordinary judicial business, but the Press Ombudsman would have the necessary authority and experience to decide such disputed classification questions as would arise from time to time were a Freedom of Information Act to be placed on the statute books. He might also be asked to supervise civil-service decisions to withhold documents for more than thirty years under the Public Records Act.

The scheme outlined above derives in part from a tried and tested method of administrative control. The Press Ombudsman would be a creature of neither parliament nor the press. He or she would have no power of 'censorship' whatsoever: the only statutory force available would be to order corrections of proven falsehoods. The great advantage of the system for the press would be to relieve it of much of the legal game of bluff and counterbluff which goes on at present in libel litigation, attended by heavy legal costs and the risk of heavy damages. This relief might prove so welcome that many journals would wish to 'contract in' to a scheme which would offer them a better and cheaper form of libel insurance than they could otherwise hope to obtain. On the other hand, victims of factual errors would have a speedy and certain remedy were the editor to refuse them a correction or reply, and the very existence of a Press Ombudsman would make unreasonable refusals by editors much less common. The victims of deliberate and malicious falsehoods would retain, as a last resort, the right to sue for damages, a right which would be extended, through legal aid, to all members of society.

The Ombudsman and the right of reply In the scheme outlined above, the Press Ombudsman would have the power to direct publication of a statement of reasonable length replying to editorials or feature articles which had made comments critical of the complainant on the basis of facts falsely or misleadingly stated. This would provide a limited legal right of reply, which would remedy the most damaging kinds of erroneous comment. Is there any need to go further, and to provide an enforceable right to reply to attacks made by way of argument or abuse or exaggeration, which may be wounding and defamatory yet contain no demonstrable factual mistake? Western European press laws do permit replies in such circumstances. The West

German law, for example, allows a person attacked in the press to obtain a court order for publication of a counter-statement, although the court does not investigate the contents of the counter-statement, which may itself contain factual inaccuracies. The Press Council, in its formulation of the principle of the right of reply, speaks of a 'moral entitlement' which belongs to 'any person or organisation identifiably attacked', irrespective of the factual accuracy of the basis for that attack. In practice, however, its adjudications sometimes turn on the view it takes of the justice of the attack.

There can be no objection to an obligation on the press to carry reasonable responses to opinions when those opinions are based on misleading or mistaken premises. But the analysis of Press Council rulings on the more general right of reply, set out in Chapter 4, demonstrates that any broader obligation cannot be stated as a simple proposition. It would need a number of qualifications and exceptions, of a sort which could readily be incorporated into an extended code of conduct, but which would provide a lawyer's picnic if ossified in a statute. An appropriate and flexible code on the right of reply should be drafted and updated by a reformed Press Council, leaving the Ombudsman to enforce a right to reply only to opinions based on mis-stated facts. It would be possible, however, to achieve a measure of collaboration between the two bodies. If the statute creating the Ombudsman's office empowered him, additionally, to direct publication of a reply according to principles from time to time declared by the Press Council, the two goals (i.e. a sensible code on the subject and a measure of speedy enforcement of the right) could be secured. If this course were to be taken, it should carry the same legal consequence for the newspaper as a direction to correct a factual error, namely, relief from a libel action in respect of the original publication.

Further reform of the libel law An alternative practical basis for encouraging a right of reply to defamatory attacks which do not contain demonstrable errors of fact could be achieved by further reform of the libel law. It is not widely recognized that a legal right of reply has existed, in a limited form, in English law ever since 1881. This has been achieved by granting qualified privilege from libel suit to press reports of defamatory statements made on occasions of public importance, but only if the newspapers carrying the defamatory reports are prepared to give the persons defamed a reasonable opportunity to reply. This reform was achieved, through pressure from press interests, in 1881, when qualified privilege was extended by statute to fair and accurate reports of certain public meetings. The privilege can only be relied upon if the person defamed has been offered the opportunity to provide for publication 'a reasonable letter or statement of explanation or contradiction'.[10] In 1888 this privilege was further extended to reports of select committee hearings and to the publication of notices issued by police and by government departments.[11] The 1952 Defamation Act added to reports 'privileged subject to explanation or contradiction' accounts of the meetings and adjudications of most voluntary associations, public meetings of companies, and proceedings in Commonwealth courts.[12]

The Faulks Committee on Defamation, reporting in 1975, recommended that the privilege of reporting defamatory statements, subject to a right of reply by the person defamed, should be extended much further: to the proceedings of EEC committees, foreign courts, press conferences, statements by foreign governments, reports of the take-over panel and to all reports and adjudications issued by the Press Council.[13] These reforms have not been implemented, and newspapers have in recent years often paid heavy damages for accurate reports of statements made on occasions which would, had the Faulks proposal passed into law, have been protected by this 'right of reply' privilege. A legal right of reply to persons who have been the subject of newspaper attack could most readily be encouraged simply by extending privilege from libel action for those attacks to newspapers prepared to publish 'a reasonable statement of explanation or contradiction'. This would apply in cases where the attack, although damaging in its abuse or exaggerated argument, does not contain sufficient factual error to fall within the province of the Press Ombudsman. An extension of legal aid to support libel actions in these areas outside the Ombudsman's province would be a powerful inducement to newspaper editors to give victims of damaging personal attacks the opportunity to make counter-statements instead of proceeding with a lawsuit.

The Reformed Press Council

The creation of a statutory Press Ombudsman, and a media-wide body campaigning to extend freedom of expression, would leave the Press Council free to concern itself with the formulation and maintenance of ethical standards. This it could achieve with some degree of success under its present private structure if its sponsors were prepared not only to make more funds available and to publicize its operations, but to take the step suggested by the second Royal Commission and to bind themselves by contract to cooperate with council enquiries and to publish adjudications as directed by the council. A reformed Press Council would be distinguished from the present body by these features:

Organization A full-time chairman would be required, convening council meetings at least once each month. He would preside over regular weekly meetings, held in public whenever appropriate, of a small and expert complaints committee; its members would deserve some payment for their time-consuming service. The drawbacks of the existing thirty-six-member council have been pointed out (see p. 24); a smaller body, with lay members who are experienced at assessing evidence and promoting consumer interests would make the council stronger and more effective, especially if some were nominated by organizations like the NCCL. Within the present press allocation of eighteen seats, (reduced comparably with any reduction of lay seats), a better 'press' mix might be: four proprietors, six editors, six journalists and two representatives of the print unions. The standing committee on complaints would be serviced by a staff which would include several investigators (the job should be paid well enough to attract experienced investigative journalists). Annual reports would appear shortly after the end of the year in question, and not after a lapse of three or so years. The council would not attempt the impossible task of drawing up a code of conduct to cover every eventuality, but in those areas where a clear code is both practicable and desirable, the council would formulate its principles and publish them in booklets explaining, by reference to decided cases, its applications of those principles. The council's sponsors must agree to advertise the council's services by donating newspaper space: a quarter-page every month in every national and provincial newspaper would not be an insupportable burden.

Monitoring and investigating The council would be much more active in monitoring the press, and in drawing attention to breaches of standards which had not been raised by individual complainants. Where individual complaints raise substantive general issues rather than personal grievances, the complaints committee should take over the matter and investigate for itself, rather than merely sitting back to adjudicate between two sides unequal in power and resources.

At present, the Press Council compares miserably with the Advertising Standards Authority, which employs three case officers who are engaged full-time in across-the-board scanning of newspapers and magazines. All national daily papers are 'vetted' every fourth issue, all national Sunday papers are scrutinized on two issues out of three, and a selection of the provincial and periodical press is scrutinized in rotation. This department was set up in 1978, after the Director-General of Fair Trading had observed that 'the processing of complaints is no substitute for a properly planned programme of monitoring work'. [14] In 1981 the monitoring department turned up about 300 breaches of the advertising code: a reassurance to the public both that breaches were likely to be located and dealt with, and that breaches of the ASA's code, given the large number of publications monitored, were comparatively rare. [15] Unless the Press Council is given the resources to follow the ASA's lead, it will be unable to rebut the criticism that its Declarations of Principle are regularly and brazenly broken.

Adjudications Criticisms of the present procedure, together with detailed proposals for reform, are set out in the conclusion to Chapter 3. The reformed council will have to find ways to overcome the delay and the procedural obstacles revealed by the consumer survey which forms the basis of that chapter. The existence of a standing complaints committee and a team of investigators would be a pre-condition for effective work, together with a move away from adversary procedures towards an inquisitional role. It will also need to improve the quality of the reasoning in its adjudications, if these are to form the basis of acceptable codes of conduct for the press.

As a complement to its monitoring work, the council should issue regular assessments of the performance of the press in complying with its major Declarations of Principle. It might take up one valuable suggestion, made in *The Times* editorial published on the day of the parliamentary debate over Frank Allaun's 'Right of Reply' Bill:

> It is worth thousands more pounds of British newspaper money to equip a Press Council to carry out an authoritative role of supervision – even of audit – of the activities of newspapers, in order to avoid a statutory alternative. A useful

procedure might indeed be an annual audit of each national and major provincial newspaper by a properly equipped Press Council research team briefing the full Council so that it could engage the editor in a formal hearing rather like a Select Committee. Editors are currently responsible in law for the contents of their papers, and to the board of their companies for its general editorial management. It is often lonely in the editorial chair, but public accountability before a body such as the Press Council would bring conviction, and its prospect, each year, would also instil a sense of proportion into editorial decisions which not only Mr Allaun has perceived to be inconsistent with the high standards required if a free press want to remain free.[16]

An annual Press Council audit of the ethical performance of newspapers would assume considerable importance if amendments were made to the Companies Acts to require newspaper groups to publish the results of the audit in their annual reports. Just as they are presently required to disclose contributions made to political parties, so they could be required to publicize the Press Council's view of their contribution to the standing of the British press. If the Press Council were additionally obliged to report to the Monopolies Commission on the ethical record of newspapers controlled by any proprietor who was seeking to enlarge his press holdings, there would be a real commercial incentive for newspaper organizations to ensure that their papers took heed of council adjudications.

Enforcement of rulings The Press Council would remain a voluntary body, dependent upon persuasion rather than law to promote compliance with its codes. However, in order that its adjudications should carry some persuasive force, the council must be in a position to ensure that they receive proper and public attention. The alternative to legal regulation was suggested by the second Royal Commission on the Press: it must take the form of contracts entered into between major newspaper publishers and the council, whereby the publishers undertake to publish adjudications with a degree of prominence dictated by the council itself.[17] If a complaint against a front-page splash story is upheld, the newspaper may at present weasel out of what is no more than a 'moral duty' by burying the embarrassing adjudication, in small type or in truncated form, on an inside page. In such cases, the council must insist that due prominence is given to its decision, if necessary by directing a front-page summary and a full report in the news section. The newspaper would remain free, of course, to disagree with the verdict in its editorial columns, but it must be under an obligation to carry the judgement in full so that its readers can make up their own minds. The episode of the *Sun* and the Deptford protest adjudication, in which the newspaper mis-reported the adjudication in the course of attacking the council and its complainants, should never be allowed to recur.

A contractual obligation to publish as directed by the council would be specifically enforceable by a court order. Alternatively, each contract with the council could specify a sum of 'liquidated damages' to be paid by the newspaper if it failed to obey a council directive to publish the adjudication. This sum could be fixed at a level which would supply the council with sufficient funds to take advertising space – in rival newspapers, and even on television – to publicize its unpublished adjudication. This would provide the council with the teeth it needs to combat the threat, made by the *News of the World* newspaper in 1982, that it would refuse to publish an adjudication which criticized its reporters. If *News of the World* readers were not permitted to read the adjudication in their newspaper, they could be made aware of it by radio and television announcements, paid for by the *News of the World* under the damages clause of its contract with the council.

A Press Council which took active steps to promulgate authoritative and acceptable codes of ethical conduct should support action to endorse those codes by sections within the industry. For example, it should support journalists who are prepared to resist editorial pressures to behave unethically. According to the council's report on 'Press Conduct in the Sutcliffe Case', some of the journalists who 'ferociously and callously' invaded the privacy of the grieving parents of a 'Ripper' victim expressed a sense of shame at their behaviour, but maintained that they were obliged to carry out their editor's instructions.[18] The Press Council must protect any journalist against editorial reprisals for refusing instructions of this sort. It should insist that publishers incorporate, in all contracts with employees, a conscience clause to the effect that no journalist can be obliged to act in breach of a Press Council Declaration of Principle. In this way, any attempt by an editor to discipline or dismiss a journalist for acting in accordance with Press Council rulings would be punished by heavy awards of damages, in claims either for breach of contract or for unfair dismissal.

Training of journalists The education and training of journalists has been ignored by the Press Council since its inception. Yet it is clear that if ethical rules are to be live issues for journalists and editors, at least in the future, they must be discussed and examined in courses of study for professional qualification. At present, professional conduct is given little or no attention in training programmes. The National Council for the Training of Journalists (NCTJ) candidly admits that its course 'is not designed to give a wide or profound education, but to provide trainees with bodies of knowledge on matters connected with their work as journalists and to teach specific intellectual and physical skills'. There is no textbook on journalistic ethics, no material is supplied by the Press Council specifically for training programmes, and no body of doctrine exists in published form to alert journalists to their responsibilities to the public or to provide them with sufficient ideological backbone to withstand the pressures towards unethical behaviour. The scrawled and misspelt notes shoved under the doors of sheltering Sutcliffe's relatives offering instant fortunes for exclusive interviews, provides a sorry commentary on the moral illiteracy of some news reporters.

The first Royal Commission on the Press envisaged the Press Council as a body which would ensure that entrants to the profession received adequate academic training, and which would additionally 'assist mature journalists to study the problems of the profession and their political and economic background'.[19] In due course, the training of journalists came to be administered by the NCTJ, a body which is dominated by employers and which has no representatives of the public on its council. Its curriculum, taught at a number of colleges of further and higher education, has been criticized as narrow and unimaginative. The NCTJ was seriously affected in 1982, when the government wound up the Printing and Publishing Industries Training Board, which had been an important source of financial support. Some large newspaper companies, like Westminster Press, conduct their own in-house training schemes independently of the NCTJ.

In these circumstances, it is not practicable for the Press Council to take formal responsibility, as the first Royal Commission recommended, for the education and training of journalists. However, one development which is fundamental to the council's future is that it should be involved in formulating, teaching, examining and promoting courses on press ethics. The raw material is available, in abundance, through the 'case studies' provided by its own adjudications. It must begin to foster an appreciation of the ethical dilemmas encountered in journalism, and give trainees (and working journalists attending further education courses) sufficient material critically to appreciate its own work in the area. In 1979, Granada Television screened six seminars at which journalists and editors agonized as they would in real life over moral dilemmas encountered in their work. At none of these seminars did any participant think even to mention the existence of the Press Council.[20]

The Prospects for Reform

This chapter has argued the need for a new settlement between public and press, based on three procedural pillars:

1 Laws for the press: Law reform aimed at securing greater freedom for investigative reporting through specific legislation, which would include a Freedom of Information Act and relaxations of the laws of libel, contempt and breach of confidence.

2 A Press Ombudsman: A statutory officer, empowered to direct the publication of corrections and replies in newspapers which have failed to put right demonstrable errors of fact. The Ombudsman would in most cases replace both the law of libel and the Press Council as the method of redress for this problem.

3 A reformed Press Council: A body representative of both public and press, supporting the persuasive force of its adjudications by contractual powers to direct prominent publication in offending newspapers, together with the long-term influence which would come from published codes of conduct, monitoring and auditing, reporting to the Monopolies Commission, and responsibility for compulsory professional-conduct courses in training schemes for journalists.

It is difficult to see how such a settlement could do other than advance press freedom in Britain. The law-reform component would give the media generally more opportunity to investigate and report on matters of public interest. The Ombudsman would relieve newspapers of most threats of libel – threats which will loom very large come the inevitable day when legal aid is extended to fund defamation actions. The *quid pro quo* would be a legal duty to correct false statements – a duty which could impinge only upon the freedom to publish falsehoods. A reformed Press Council would be a deterrent to sloppy and unethical editors. Its contractual powers to direct publication of its adjudications would occasionally spoil their front pages, and they may find their journalists developing the moral muscle to resist editorial orders to intrude upon privacy when the public interest is not at stake. If the true freedom of the press lies in the right of newspapers to present the public with facts required for democratic judgement, the work of both Press Ombudsman and reformed Press Council would serve to enhance, rather to restrict, that freedom. Why, then, are these reforms likely to be opposed by many press interests and by the (unreformed) Press Council? The objection with most merit will be based on the inherent dangers of statutory intervention.

Reform by statute – or by contract? Newspapers are reluctant to submit to parliamentary reform, with some reason. The inept drafting of the Contempt of Court Act, the wrecking of the Freedom of Information Bill, and the failure to reform official secrecy and libel are all grounds for distrusting a political process which has shown scant concern in its statutes for the fine print of press freedom. An unhelpful precedent was created by the 1981 Broadcasting Act, which established a Broadcasting Complaints Commission (BCC) to adjudicate complaints against radio and television. [21] The BCC was modelled all too closely on the existing Press Council, with the result that its rulings have been dilatory and largely devoid of principle. Parliament made many mistakes in setting up the BCC, a body whose functions largely duplicate the control already exerted by the Independent Broadcasting Authority and the BBC. It opted for a tribunal empowered to decide over-broad issues ('unfair treatment' and 'invasion of privacy') through adversarial proceedings which could be brought only by 'persons aggrieved'. Its members are political appointees without special ability at fact-finding. Its procedures are complicated, it has no trained investigative staff, and it does not function as a replacement for the law of libel. Its first eighteen months of operation made little impact: eight of its eighteen cases were brought by the National Front, an organization with the experience and the dedication to overcome its procedural hurdles. It serves to irritate programme-makers without contributing to an informed debate about programme standards. As the result of a court ruling in 1982, it cannot adjudicate issues which are subject to libel proceedings – the very issues which a statutory Press Ombudsman, as envisaged above, would decide *instead* of the libel law. [22]

The Press Ombudsman would mean a new press law, albeit one with beneficent features. The propensity of politicians and parliamentary draftsmen to mishandle media legislation raises the question of whether a modified form of the Ombudsman idea could be achieved voluntarily. The Swedish Press Ombudsman derives his powers from contracts entered into by all press proprietors. In America, the *Washington Post* submits complaints from its readers to a distinguished and independent Ombudsman, whose investigations it has bound itself to assist and whose adjudications it undertakes to publish. Would the present sponsors of the Press Council, the members of the Newspaper Publishing Association and the Newspaper Society, be prepared to enter into contracts obliging their papers to accept the jurisdiction of an Ombudsman? Such contracts would be enforceable by the Ombudsman obtaining a court order for specific performance.

A scheme based on contract has one principal advantage over a statutory arrangement, in that it is voluntarily entered into, and so provides a binding system of self-discipline which the press, having set the scheme up, could hardly resent. The great attraction of a statutory scheme, on the other hand, is an advantage for the press, in that only a statute can free it from defamation actions, by requiring that libel writs be transformed into complaints to the Ombudsman. A statutory scheme would therefore be preferable, although the voluntary system which operates in Sweden does provide an example of how such a system can be made to work.

The Swedish Press Ombudsman Sweden was the first country to set up a Press Council, in 1916. By the late sixties the Swedish council came under the same sort of attack that its British equivalent is now suffering. So, in 1969, a professional judge was appointed as the first Press Ombudsman, with a full investigative staff. He monitors the press, receives all complaints against it (for breaches of ethics as well as mistakes of fact) and performs a corrective function by arranging for appropriate retractions or replies or reprimands to be published, usually within a few days. [23] The system is free to complainants, and is fully supported by the press – all newspapers (with one small-circulation exception) have bound themselves by contracts with the Press Council to submit to the Ombudsman's rulings. In complicated cases, or those which appear to involve very serious breaches of ethics, the Ombudsman may refer the matter to the Press Council – a body representative of both public and press, and chaired by another judge. If the Press Council decides to censure a newspaper, then that newspaper is obliged by the terms of its contract with the council to publish the adjudication as directed, and also to pay a fine of about £750. The third Royal Commission studied the work of the Swedish Press Ombudsman, and reported that 'we were impressed by his obvious independence and public standing and by the active help he was able to offer to complainants'. Its only reservation about importing the idea into an English context was that an Ombudsman 'would lead to a duplication of procedures' with the Press Council – he would not 'fit readily into its existing framework'.[24] As the Press Council does not have a satisfactory existing framework this reservation is groundless. A Press Ombudsman could provide speedy and effective redress for inaccuracy, leaving the council to concern itself with the question of press standards.

'Why must it always be Sweden?' is an objection (first attributed to Lord Hailsham) inevitably raised against reforming British practices upon continental examples. Although the existing British Ombudsman has Scandinavian ancestry the objection does have some point. The Swedish press was willing to enter into a binding system of self-regulation because it enjoyed, and wished to retain, freedoms which the British press does not possess. These include a wide-ranging Freedom of Information Act, and numerous laws which protect the rights of journalists. For example, no libel action may be brought by any corporation or organization, and the press is protected against suit by individuals if its defamatory statements were reasonably believed to be true, and concerned matters of public interest. Privileges of this sort are unknown to English law: they provide such a solid base for investigative reporting that the Swedish press has been willing to discipline itself in areas where the public interest is not involved.

The British press has no similar incentive. Self-discipline will not come voluntarily: it will come, if at all, churlishly and only when public outcry over behaviour of the sort revealed in the Sutcliffe case reaches such a pitch that legislation seems inevitable.

The debate in 1983 The likelihood is that self-discipline will not come at all. The chairman of the Press Council, in his foreword to the Annual Report for 1979, published in November 1982, wrote that 'I see no prospect whatever of universal consent being forthcoming from journalists, editors, proprietors and publishers for the Council to be enabled to impose penalties on a voluntary basis.'[25] The time for that consent came and went with the publication of the report on the Sutcliffe case in February 1983. Three newspapers, *The Times*, the *Guardian* and the *Financial Times*, urged their brethren to adopt stricter and more formal methods of compliance with the council, but to no avail. As the *Guardian* pointed out editorially, a fortnight after the report was published:

Things have not improved since Sutcliffe. Some things (like Miss Susan Stephens tripping away from court with the *Mail*) are exactly the same. Some things – for a beset Royal Family amongst others – are much, much worse. There may be a new law after this report. We shall resist it vigorously if there is, as there should be a free alternative. But what alternative? The background is of bitter tabloid circulation rivalry in a hard world which expects to be paid. Editors in Fleet Street compete in that world like football managers told covertly to put the boot in by their chairmen – or join the dole queue. Any real attempt to lift the pressure now – at the eleventh hour – can only come via the Newspaper Publishers' Association. If the Lords and tycoons and conglomerates who own so much of our press would agree to follow the Press Council to the letter, then that might just hold. But it is the final fix of free medicine in the Last Chance Saloon.[26]

That has been the sentiment, if not the language, of three Royal Commissions on the Press. 'Put your house in order – or else.' It is the constant cry of the chairman and the director of the Press Council: 'If you don't stick by our rulings, legislation will surely follow.' The fact that legislation never does follow must be very apparent to cynical and circulation-hungry editors.

Two weeks after the report on the Sutcliffe case, the Press Council's performance was debated in parliament in the context of an ineptly drafted 'Right of Reply' Bill. Although the second reading was supported by opposition parties and a number of back-bench Conservatives, and secured ninety votes against seven, it failed to obtain the requisite support (100 votes) necessary to go forward. The minister of state for the Home Office announced that the government would not support legislation 'until we are quite satisfied that the Press Council is not able to deal with these matters properly'.[27] He displayed a remarkable ignorance about the Council, at one stage incorrectly informing the House that 'The Hon. Gentleman will see from the reports of the Press Council that its judgements are adhered to pretty well by the Press, as they should be, given that the Council is a self-regulating body consisting in the main of professional journalists.'[28]

In a successful bid for government support in this debate, the Press Council issued a special statement which made familiar promises:

> The Council believes editors must accept the obligation to correct significant inaccuracies and to give people and organisations they attack an opportunity to reply. It agrees with the public demand for a quick procedure for dealing with requests for publication of corrections and replies to attacks.
>
> To meet this need it is extending and speeding up its conciliation service which was suggested by the Royal Commission on the Press and has been well used, and is considering another 'fast track' option under which the Council's director or a small panel will rule swiftly on calls for corrections or a right of reply from people or organisations about whom news or articles are published.

The 'well used' conciliation service was used only seventeen times in 1979, the most recent year for which figures are available. A 'fast track' option had been promised to the Royal Commission in 1975, to the TUC in August 1982, and to the public in regular press statements over the years. At the time it gave this new assurance to the government, in February 1983, the council was still considering how to rule on a call to correct a bogus interview with the widow of a Falklands hero, published in the *Sun* four months previously. The 'fast track' option – of picking up a telephone and asking the widow whether she had given the interview – had not been exercised.

Conclusion

This study began by assessing the performance of the Press Council in living up to its stated objectives. The final chapter has necessarily examined some aspects of libel law, and the experiences of other Western countries in finding alternative mechanisms to correct press distortion. The tripartite settlement which has been advocated – laws to open up areas of investigative reporting, a Press Ombudsman to correct demonstrable errors, and a Press Council with certain contractual powers over newspapers, will be decried in some quarters as a restraint on editorial freedom and in others as an over-tolerant and legalistic approach to abuses of that freedom. A more compelling comment may be that these reforms are not sufficiently far-reaching to comprehend the future of media technology. The electronic revolution has thrown up powerful forms of communication which are outside the scope of this study; regulatory systems will need to encompass telecommunications as well as print. That would mean extensive parliamentary select committee hearings as a prelude to a basic media law, which would cover not only legal and ethical standards but associated questions of training, finance, advertising and new technologies. The result might then be a legislative package which could incorporate a media Ombudsman in the course of a wider arrangement, which could include freedom of information provisions and relief from the more onerous duties of libel, contempt and confidence.

However, the stumbling block of principle to any new settlement between the media and the public appears to be an ill-considered passage in the report of the third Royal Commission on the Press, elevated to the status of government policy in the 1983 'Right of Reply' debate. [29] After favourably considering the working of continental press laws, which provide both written guarantees of press freedom together with rights of privacy and rights of reply, the Royal Commission baulked at the introduction of such a settlement in Britain:

> We believe that the press should not be subjected to a special regime of law, and that it should neither have special privileges nor labour under special disadvantages compared with the ordinary citizen. That argues against a special measure for ensuring a right of reply. We prefer a non-legal method securing corrections. [30]

This argument is riddled with mistakes:
- *The press should not be subjected to a special regime of law.* The press is already subjected to special legal regimes. The laws which deal with copyright, contempt, defamation, court reporting, rehabilitation of offenders, official secrecy, elections, local council meetings, matrimonial proceedings, race relations – to

name but a few – have special provisions applying only to the media.

● *The press should not have special privileges.* The press already has some special privileges, and it needs more. Journalists have, for example, the privilege of remaining in certain courts and meetings when members of the public have been excluded, and the privilege of declining to answer courtroom questions which would reveal the identity of a source, when 'ordinary citizens' would be guilty of contempt for a refusal to answer.[31]

● *There should be no special legal measure for securing corrections.* A special and legal measure for securing corrections already exists, namely, the law of defamation.

From premises which are factually incorrect, the commission leaps to a conclusion which is patently absurd. The idea that newspapers must have no privileges not available to the ordinary citizen overlooks the fact that ordinary citizens do not own newspapers. And it is those ordinary citizens who are placed at a special disadvantage when attacked by newspapers they do not own. The Royal Commission has formulated a nonsensical proposition, which the government has accepted, to define the relationship between the people and the press.

That relationship needs more careful consideration. If the freedom of the press is truly a freedom to provide the facts necessary for democratic choice, the press requires certain privileges to enable it to obtain and to publish those facts. Such privileges would include a Freedom of Information Act and a lifting of some of the existing legal restrictions on the publication of information of public interest. In return for these privileges, there is no reason in principle why the press should not be given corresponding duties to ensure that factual errors are corrected, that privacy is not invaded in order to obtain stories of no importance, and that certain ethical standards are generally observed. The press requires privileges in order to serve the public interest; if, in the course of exercising these privileges, it should unfairly attack ordinary citizens, the public interest is served by affording its victims an effective right to set the record straight. The press itself, through the council which it funds for the purpose, has failed to secure this right for the disadvantaged citizen. Parliament, through its responsibility for law reform, has failed to secure necessary rights for the press. The time has come for both Estates to agree on a better system of management.

158

Appendix A
Evidence from Complainants

The following individuals and organizations supplied written evidence and comments to the author concerning their experiences of Press Council procedures:

R. Adams
Aims of Industry
David Anderson (Ex-editor,
    Eton Chronicle)
Association of Scientific,
    Technical and Managerial
    Staff
Ken Aston

Basildon Council (Town
    Manager)
J. D. Beanse
C. I. Boswell

Lady Colin Campbell
Centre for Contemporary
    Studies (Eric Moonman)
The Civil Service Union
County of Cambridgeshire,
    Social Services Department

Eric Deakins MP
Derbyshire County Council

Embassy of Pakistan
E. F. Earwaker

The Farm and Food Society
Federation of Claimants Union
John Foster
W. R. Foster
Paul Francis

Ralph Glasser
Golders Green Unitarians
Kenneth Grant

The Harris Tweed Association
    Ltd
Harrow Council (Department
    of Law and Administration)
Dorothy Harwood
J. W. Hepting
Denis Hullah

W. R. L. Jones

Graeme Kidd
Esme Kirby

Liberal Party Organization
F. Liesching
Mary Littledale
V. Lydon

Patrick MacPhail
Tony Marlow MP
Hugh McCartney MP
R. D. Miller
MIND (Tony Smythe)
B. S. Michin
Penelope Money-Coutts
G. C. Morris
M. B. Moulder
Musicians' Union

The National Theatre
The Naturist Foundation
Desmond
   Nethersole-Thompson

Alison M. Oliver
J. L. Oxlade

Jeff Pirie
R. J. Pritchard
The Pro-Life Information
   Centre
J. K. Purves

Nick Raynsford

Stella Richter
Dr Violet Rowe

Sappho
Arthur Scargill
Mark Sealey
Sefton Area Health Authority
Shelter
D. Shepherd
Brian C. Smith
Dorothy Smythe
Peter Snape MP
Blaine Stothard

W. J. Taylor
Martin Tucker

L. A. Verity

Richard Wainwright MP
Wakefield Council
L. E. Weidberg
Norman Welch
Michael Willey
Leslie Woodhead

Appendix B
Members of the Enquiry

SARAH BOSTON is a freelance film director and writer. As a director she has worked for the BBC, ITV and Channel 4. Her published work includes two books, *Women Workers and the Trade Unions* and *Will, My Son*. She is also a member of the Association of Cinematograph, Television and Allied Technicians, and has served eight years on the executive committee, two of them as vice-president.

GEOFFREY DRAIN is general secretary of NALGO (National and Local Government Officers' Association), a position he has held since 1973. He is a barrister, a magistrate, a member of the General Council of the TUC, and a director of the Bank of England. He serves on a number of government committees dealing with law, finance and local government.

JACOB ECCLESTONE is the deputy general secretary of the National Union of Journalists. He worked for many years as a journalist on *The Times*. He was a member of the Press Council between 1977 and 1980.

GEOFFREY GOODMAN is a journalist, author and broadcaster; and assistant editor and industrial editor of the *Daily Mirror*. He was a member of the third Royal Commission on the Press, and joint author with David Basnett of the Minority Report in that commission. He was head of the Counter-inflation Unit, 1975–6.

RICHARD HOGGART is Warden of Goldsmiths College and a governor of the Royal Shakespeare Theatre. He served on the Pilkington Committee on Broadcasting, and was chairman of the

New Statesman and vice-chairman of the Arts Council. His books include *The Uses of Literacy* (1957), *Speaking to Each Other* (1970) and *Only Connect* (the 1971 Reith lectures).

JOHN MONKS is a trade union official and a former journalist on newspapers and radio. He is a district officer for NALGO and has run specialist courses for trade unionists on ownership and control of the media and the right of reply.

RUSSELL PROFITT is principal race relations adviser to Brent Borough Council, and was formerly deputy head of a Deptford primary school. He has been a local councillor in Lewisham for seven years, and is involved in a number of community groups.

GEOFFREY ROBERTSON is a barrister and author. His publications include *Reluctant Judas* (1976), *Obscenity* (1979) and *Law for the Press* (1978). In 1980 he was a visiting fellow at Warwick University, and in 1982 he wrote and presented the Granada television series *Tree of Liberty*. He is the editor of 'Out of Court', the *Guardian*'s legal column, and chairman of the Radio 4 programme *You the Jury*.

MURIEL TURNER is assistant general secretary of the Association of Scientific, Technical and Managerial Staffs (ASTMS), a position held since 1971. She holds one of the five women's seats on the TUC General Council, and is a member of the TUC Media Committee. She is a member of the Equal Opportunities Commission.

PHILLIP WHITEHEAD is MP for Derby North, and Labour's spokesman on higher education and the arts. He is a writer and broadcaster, who produced 'This Week' for Thames Television from 1967 to 1970, and served on the Annan Committee on the Future of Broadcasting. He was chairman of the Fabian Society in 1978–9 and is currently on the Council of the Consumers' Association.

KATHARINE WHITEHORN is an associate editor and columnist on the *Observer*. She has worked for a variety of papers including *Picture Post, Woman's Own* and the *Spectator*. She is currently the president of the Open Section of the Royal Society of Medicine and Rector of St Andrew's University.

Appendix C
Other Organizations

Organizations which have an interest in some of the questions canvassed in this book include:

The Advertising Standards Authority
A body established and funded by the advertising industry to supervise a system of self-regulation for public advertising. It investigates complaints from members of the public that particular advertisements are in breach of the British Code of Advertising Practice, and operates a monitoring system to ensure compliance with the code. Its slogan – 'legal, decent, honest and truthful' is promoted in space donated by newspapers, whose publishers undertake not to carry advertisements which have been held by the ASA to be in breach of the code.
Chairman: Lord Macgregor. Address: Brook House, 2–16 Torrington Place, London WC1.

The Broadcasting Complaints Commission
A statutory body set up by parliament in 1981 to consider and adjudicate complaints of 'unjust or unfair treatment' in programmes broadcast on radio and television, and 'unwarranted infringement of privacy in, or in connection with, the obtaining of material included in programmes'. It can require the attendance of broadcasters in the course of its investigations, and has power to order that the result of its adjudications are broadcast in a manner appropriate to redress the original unfairness. It operates in addition to controls exerted by the BBC and the IBA, and its work since its inception has been unimpressive.
Chairman: Lady Pike. Address: 20 Albert Embankment, London SW1.

The Campaign for Press and Broadcasting Freedom

The Campaign for Press and Broadcasting Freedom, which initiated this report, is one of the few organizations which has attempted to focus public attention on the Press Council. The campaign was set up in 1979 as a broad-based, non-party organization with members and affiliates from all walks of life.

The campaign's statement of aims commits it to working for a 'reformed and reconstituted Press Council to promote basic standards of fairness and access to the press on behalf of the public'. The principle of the 'right of reply' is also fundamental to redressing imbalance in the press, it states.

The campaign is also committed to challenging the consensus notions of 'impartiality', 'balance' and 'freedom' in the broadcasting and newspaper media, believing that changes in the structures of ownership and control are necessary in order to provide genuine freedom, diversity and access.

Support for community-based and 'alternative' newspapers, the right of access to the wholesale newspaper distribution network, freedom-of-information legislation and industrial democracy within the media industries are also part of the campaign's objectives.

Secretary: John Jennings, Address: 9 Poland Street, London, W1.

Guild of British Newspaper Editors

A body representing editors, mainly those working on provincial newspapers. It makes submissions to government bodies and issues statements from time to time in support of press freedom and editorial independence. It lacks the resources to campaign, although it does hold a joint annual conference with the Law Society at which legal topics of current concern to the media are discussed.

Secretary: Nicholas Herbert.

International Freedom of Information Institute

Acts as an international clearing house for information on all aspects of freedom of information, and publishes a regular news-letter on the subject.

Secretary: Tom Riley. Address: 76 Shoe Lane, London EC4.

Institute of Journalists

A member and supporter of the Press Council, although it has called for a stronger professional association with powers to suspend and expel journalists. It operates as a trade union for journalists dissatisfied with the NUJ, and currently has about 2500 members. It occasionally speaks out on press-freedom issues, but does not support its arguments with publications of any significance.

Secretary: Robert Farmer. Address: Bedford Chambers, Covent Garden, WC2.

International Press Institute

This organization does valuable work in training journalists from third-world countries and in protecting foreign correspondents from government reprisals. Its British section organizes occasional seminars and debates on topics of current concern to the local media.

Chairman of British Executive: Frank Rogers. Address: City University, John Street, EC1.

The Media Society

An organization mainly composed of journalists and newspaper lawyers, which holds three or four meetings a year on subjects of mutual interest, such as contempt, official secrecy and cheque-book journalism.

Secretary: John Corrie, *Daily Mirror*

National Council for Civil Liberties

The pressure group which has been most active in recent years on press-freedom issues. It lobbies MPs, issues detailed analysis of impending legislation which might threaten the media, and publishes booklets on freedom of information, contempt, privacy and the like. Its legal department has taken up and conducted several test cases on behalf of press interests, sometimes in conjunction with the NUJ. Membership is open to the public.

General Secretary: Patricia Hewitt. Address: 21 Tabard Street, SE1.

The National Union of Journalists

The dominant trade union for journalists, it has a membership of 32,000, and speaks out aggressively on press-freedom issues. It withdrew from the Press Council in 1980, declaring that organization 'incapable of reform'. Although it has not formulated proposals for a replacement, it does offer members of the public an alternative method of complaining about journalists' conduct. The complaint will go before the branch of which the journalist is a member, and may lead to disciplinary action at a local level if deemed sufficiently serious. The union has a code of conduct which sets out ethical standards binding on members in the course of their work. The code itself is impressive: attempts to enforce it have been less so.

General Secretary: Ken Ashton. Address: Acorn House, Gray's Inn Road, WC1.

References

NB 'The Press and the People' is the annual report of the Press Council.

Introduction

1 *Labour's Plan* (Labour Party 1983), p. 26.
2 'Shirley Williams in Press Council Attack', *UK Press Gazette*, 26 October 1981.
3 'Press Curb Proposal', Letter to *The Times*, dated 6 March 1981.
4 *The Media and Political Violence* (Macmillan 1981), pp. 161 *et seq.*
5 'Paper They Can't Gag', *Sun*, 8 October 1982.
6 John Junor, 'Current Events', *Sunday Express*, 3 September 1978.
7 Sir David English, 'Decision that Shackles Freedom', *Daily Mail*, 4 February 1983.
8 H. Phillip Levy, *The Press Council – History, Procedure and Cases* (Macmillan 1967).
9 Royal Commission on the Press, Cmnd. 6810 (1977), Chapter 20. paragraph 12.
10 *Ibid.*, paragraph 64.

1. Press Council History

1 Royal Commission on the Press, Cmnd. 7700 (1949).
2 *Ibid.*, paragraph 650.
3 The Press Council Bill had its second reading in November 1952. It was moved by C. J. Simmons MP, who reminded the House that 'Nearly three and a half years after [the Royal Commission report] we are still awaiting its formation by the Press of their own volition'. See, generally, Levy, *The Press Council* (Macmillan 1967), Chapters 1 and 2.
4 'A Royal Romance: Princess Margaret and Group-Captain Townsend', *Daily Mirror*, 21 February 1954 (Press Council).

5   Royal Commission on the Press, Cmnd. 1811 (1962), paragraph 325.
6   Report of the Committee on Privacy, Cmnd. 5012 (1972), paragraph 189.
7   Royal Commission on the Press, Cmnd. 6810 (1977), Chapter 20 paragraph 15.
8   *Ibid.*, paragraph 48.
9   *Ibid.*, paragraphs 51–9.
10 *Ibid.*, paragraph 77.
11 *Ibid.*, paragraphs 69 and 71.
12 'TUC Success on Press Council', *UK Press Gazette*, 30 August 1982, p. 11.
13 Patrick Wintour, *New Statesman*, 3 September 1982, p. 5.
14 Hansard, 18 February 1983, HC No. 62, Column 628.
15 'The Press and the People' (1979), foreword by Patrick Neill QC. p. 4.

2. The Council at Work

1   'The Press and the People' (1979), foreword by Patrick Neill QC, p. 153.
2   *Ibid.*, p. 3.
3   The Advertising Standards Authority: Annual Report (1981), p. 5.
4   Royal Commission on the Press, Cmnd. 6810 (1977), Chapter 20 paragraph 24.
5   'Press Council Member is Reported to the Council', *UK Press Gazette*, 15 February 1982, p. 11.
6   'Press Councillor Who Spoke Out is Barred from Legal Complaints', *UK Press Gazette*, 15 March 1982, p. 27.
7   'The Press and the People' (1979), p. 33 (P6836) and p. 44 (Q7088).
8   'The Press and the People' (1978), p. 70 (P6506) and p. 91 (P6266).
9   'Press Conduct in the Sutcliffe Case' (Press Council 1983), Chapter 17, especially paragraphs 44 and 108.
10 'Guidance on Procedure for Complainants', Press Council leaflet 109 (7th Revision, 1980).
11 'The Press and the People' (1979), p. 6.
12 Figures supplied by the Press Council to the Industry and Trade Committee of the House of Commons, Memorandum 278/351/ D1827, April 1980.
13 Letter to President of National Union of Journalists, 20 March 1980.
14 Press Council, Waiver Form, C101/67.
15 Report of the Committee on the Future of Broadcasting, Cmnd.

6733 (1977), Chapter 6 paragraph 18.

16 Royal Commission on the Press, *op. cit.*, paragraphs 43–9.

17 *Ibid.*, paragraph 45.

18 *Raymond v Honey* (1982), 1 AII ER 756.

19 Letter from assistant secretary of Press Council to Mr B. S. Minchin, 6 April, 1977.

20 Royal Commission on the Press, *op. cit.*, paragraph 58.

21 'The Press and the People' (1978), p. 3.

22 *Ibid.*

23 Memorandum to Industry and Trade Committee, April 1980, paragraph 49.

24 'Press Conduct in the Sutcliffe Case' (Press Council 1983).

25 'Press Conduct in the Thorpe Affair' (Press Council 1980), Booklet No 6.

26 'Press Conduct in the Lambton Affair' (Press Council 1973), Booklet No 5.

27 Noel S. Paul, 'Why the British Press Council Works', *Columbia Journalism Review,* Vol. 10, No. 6, p. 26.

28 Letter from Kenneth Morgan to D. Shepherd, 18 September 1980.

3. Public Complaints

1 Noel S. Paul, in 'The Press and the People' (1978), p. 6.

2 'Newspaper Stoppages', in 'The Press and the People' (1977), p. 105.

3 Memorandum of evidence to third Royal Commission by the Press Council. Answers to first and second questionnaire, and see transcript of evidence, meeting of Royal Commission on 10 October 1976.

4 'Severest Censure for Sensationalism', Adjudication 05810, in 'The Press and the People' (1977), p. 54. See also 'The Press and the People' (1979), p. 23.

5 Correspondence with author, 1 July 1981.

6 'Misleading, Careless, but not Deliberately Distorted', Adjudication 05807, in 'The Press and the People' (1978), p. 42.

7 Correspondence with author, 11 August 1981.

8 Adjudication 07336, in 'The Press and the People' (1980).

9 Letter from assistant secretary of Press Council to D. Harwood, 18 October 1979.

10 Correspondence with author, 19 August 1981 and 11 September 1981.

11 'Failed to Correct Misleading Adjudication', Adjudication P6490, in 'The Press and the People' (1979), p. 19.

12 Ros Franey, correspondence with author, 27 July 1981.
13 Adjudication Q7425, in 'The Press and the People' (1980), and correspondence with author, 18 August 1981.
14 'An Unjustified Conclusion', Adjudication A7246, in 'The Press and the People' (1979), p. 48. Correspondence, 1 July 1981.
15 'Improper Journalism by Innuendo', Adjudication P6812, *ibid.*
16 'Porno Film Complaints', *UK Press Gazette,* 4 May 1981. Correspondence, 8 July 1981.
17 Cartoon 'Outraged Decency', Adjudication P6536, in 'The Press and the People' (1978), p. 101.
18 Correspondence with author, 15 July 1981.
19 'Headline Gave Tendentious Slant', Adjudication 05320R, in 'The Press and the People' (1977), p. 42.
20 'Subterfuge was Improper', Adjudication P6279 in 'The Press and the People' (1979), p. 68. Correspondence, 16 July 1981.
21 'Five Paragraphs would have Sufficed', Adjudication 05695 in 'The Press and the People' (1977), p. 99. Correspondence, 2 July 1981.
22 Correspondence with author, 14 July and 11 September 1981. See *News of the World* report of adjudication, 17 August 1980.
23 'Newspaper and Complainant Criticised', Adjudication 05595 in 'The Press and the People' (1977), p. 55. Correspondence, 6 July and 24 August 1981.
24 'Surname Used Despite Request', Adjudication P6481 in 'The Press and the People' (1978), p. 111. Correspondence, 24 August 1981.
25 'Deplorable Personal Attack', Adjudication 05501 in 'The Press and the People' (1978), p. 51. Correspondence, 4 August 1981.
26 'Context Objectionable to Complainant', Adjudication P6836P in 'The Press and the People' (1979), p. 33. Correspondence, 3 August 1981.
27 'No Time to Comment', *UK Press Gazette,* 18 February 1980. Correspondence, 21 July 1981.
28 'Identifying Doctor had Racial Connotation', Adjudication P6451R in 'The Press and the People' (1978), p. 95. Correspondence, 2 July (Denis Hullah), 31 July and 2 September 1981.
29 Correspondence with author, 3 July 1981. See Adjudication R7776, in 'The Press and the People' (1980).
30 'Gruesome Pictures – Two Newspapers Censured', Adjudications P6554P/P6557P in 'The Press and the People' (1978), p. 102. Correspondence, 1 July 1980.
31 Correspondence with author, 10 July and 27 August 1981.
32 *Ibid.,* 27 July 1981.

33 *Ibid.*, 6 July 1981.
34 *Ibid.*, 14 August 1981.
35 *Ibid.*, 7 July and 28 August 1981.
36 *Ibid.*, 1 July 1981.
37 *Ibid.*, 1 July 1981.
38 Adjudication Q7006 in 'The Press and the People' (1980). Correspondence, 2 July and 2 October 1981.
39 Letter from Kenneth Morgan to Frank Field MP, 18 March 1980.
40 Memorandum CCC 190, 'Personal Attendances', July 1979.
41 Letter from Kenneth Morgan to J. K. Purves, 9 September 1981.

4. Professional Standards

1 Report of the Committee on Privacy, Cmnd. 5012 (1972), paragraph 147.
2 Royal Commission on the Press, Cmnd. 6810 (1977), Chapter 2 paragraph 3.
3 Adjudication Q7174, in 'The Press and the People' (1980).
4 Letter from David English to F. G. Byrne, 26 March 1980.
5 Letter from Mary Cross (assistant secretary, Press Council) to Blaine Stothard, 21 March 1980.
6 'The Press and the People' (1977), p. 72.
7 Royal Commission on the Press, *op. cit.*, Chapter 20 paragraph 67.
8 Adjudication issued on 8 October 1982.
9 'Notes Support the Accuracy', *UK Press Gazette*, 9 August 1982, p. 12.
10 Evidence to third Royal Commission on the Press submitted by Alexander Irvine in 1975.
11 Royal Commission on the Press, *op. cit.*, Chapter 20 paragraph 65.
12 'Press Conduct in the Thorpe Affair', (Press Council 1980), Booklet No. 6 paragraph 123.
13 'Press Council in the Sutcliffe Case' (Press Council 1983), Chapter 15 paragraphs 1–5.
14 *Distillers Co. (Biochemicals) Ltd v Times Newspapers Ltd* (1975), QB 613.
15 See *R. v Ameer & Lucas* (1974), Crim. LR 104.
16 'Press Conduct in the Sutcliffe Case', *op. cit.*, Chapter 15 paragraphs 5–10.
17 'When the Public's Interest Outweighs the Public Interest', *Daily Express*, 4 February 1983.
18 'Press Conduct in the Sutcliffe Case', *op. cit.*, Chapter 16 paragraph 47.
19 *Ibid.*, paragraph 81.

20   *Ibid.*, paragraph 96.
21   *Ibid.*, paragraph 112.
22   'The Press and the People' (1978), p. 3.
23   *Ibid.*, p. 39; (1979), pp. 72 and 85.
24   'No Automatic Right of Reply', Adjudication in 'The Press and the People' (1981).
25   'The Press and the People' (1977), p. 99.
26   Complaint to Press Council, 1981.
27   'The Press and the People' (1978), p. 28.
28   *Ibid.*, p. 34; (1979), p. 47.
29   *Ibid.*, p. 52.
30   *Ibid.*, p. 87.
31   *Ibid.*, p. 80.
32   'The Press and the People' (1979), p. 11.
33   'The Press and the People' (1978), p. 60.
34   *Ibid.*, p. 67.
35   *Ibid.*, p. 82.
36   *Ibid.*, p. 75.
37   *The Journalist* (Australia), July 1978, p. 2.
38   'The Press and the People' (1979), pp. 19, 35, 36, 39, 45, 48.
39   See 'Interference with Newspaper Content', *UK Press Gazette,* October 1982, p. 3; and 'Renewed Warning on Press Censorship', 'The Press and the People' (1977), p. 105.
40   Charles Wintour, 'Rights and Wrongs of a Right of Reply', the *Observer,* 1982.
41   'The Press and the People' (1977), p. 4.
42   'The Press and the People' (1979), p. 57.
43   'Pictures of Princess Brought Discredit on British Press', *UK Press Gazette,* 8 March 1982, p. 6.
44   *UK Press Gazette,* 16 August 1982.
45   'People under Pressure', Press Council, 1980.
46   'Press Conduct in the Sutcliffe Case', *op. cit.,* Chapter 18 paragraph 22.
47   *Ibid.*, paragraph 29.
48   'The Press and the People' (1977).
49   Raymond Wacks, *The Protection of Privacy* (Sweet and Maxwell, 1980), pp. 91–4.
50   H. Phillip Levy, *The Press Council* (Macmillan 1967), Preface.
51   'Press Conduct in the Sutcliffe Case', *op. cit.,* Chapter 16 paragraphs 35–49.
52   *Ibid.*, paragraphs 60–82.
53   *Ibid.*, paragraphs 91–8.
54   *Ibid.*, Chapter 17 paragraphs 39–112.

55   *Ibid.*, Chapter 16 paragraphs 7–20.
56. 'What the Papers Pay', 'World in Action', 14 March 1983 (Granada Television). See 'Ripper Case Page Reopens', *UK Press Gazette*, 21 March 1983, p. 5.
57   'Press Conduct in the Sutcliffe Case', *op. cit.*, Chapter 17 paragraph 112.
58   *Ibid.*, Chapter 1 paragraph 43.
59   *Ibid.*, Chapter 11 paragraph 12.

5. Freedom of the Press

1   'The Aberfan Inquiry and Contempt of Court' (Press Council 1967).
2   Report of Committee on the Law of Contempt as it Affects Tribunals of Inquiries, Cmnd. 4078 (1969).
3   'Privacy, Press and Public' (Press Council 1971), Booklet No. 2; 'Reforming the Law of Defamation' (Press Council 1973), Booklet No. 4.
4   Andrew Nicol, 'Official Secrets and Jury Vetting' (1979), Crim. LR 284. And see statement by the Attorney General (then Sir Hartley Shawcross QC) on the restricted scope of Section 1 in *Hansard*, 29 January 1951, Column 683.
5   'The Press and the People' (1978), p. 139.
6   *Attorney General v The Leveller* (1979), AC 440.
7   'The Press and the People' (1979), p. 112.
8   James Michael, *The Politics of Secrecy* (Penguin 1982), Chapter 11.
9   'The Press and the People' (1979), p. 108.
10   *Ibid.*, p. 109.
11   See James Michael, *op cit*. The full list of legislation which restricts the disclosure of information in the UK is set out in the Appendix to Delbridge and Smith (eds), *Consuming Secrets*, (Burnett Books 1982).
12   House of Commons Defence Committee, 3rd Report, 1979–80, 'The D Notice System', HC. 773.
13   Robert Harris, *Gotcha! The Media, the Government and the Falklands Crisis.* Faber 1983), p. 143
14   Modern Public Records (1981) Cmnd. 8204; White Paper Response (1982) Cmnd. 8531; See 'State Secrecy and Public Records', State Research Bulletin No. 30, p. 128 (1982).
15   'The Press and the People' (1958), p. 39; Report of the Departmental Committee on Proceedings before Examining Justices, Cmnd. 479 (1958).
16   Report of the Committee on Defamation, Cmnd. 5909 (1975).
17   'Breach of Confidence', The Law Commission (1981).

18 Report of the Committee to Consider the Law on Copyright and Designs, chaired by Mr Justice Whitford, (HMSO 1977), Cmnd. 6732. See especially Chapter 14.

19 'The Press and the People' (1977), p. 120.

20 Companies Act (1981), Sections 6–8.

21 HMSO (1979), Cmnd. 6888.

22 Local Government Planning and Land Act (1980).

23 *Whitehouse v Lemon* (1979) AC 617.

24 Report of the Committee on Obscenity and Film Censorship, Cmnd. 7772, 1979).

25 'Criminal Libel', Law Commission Working Paper No. 84 (1982).

26 'The Press and the People' (1971), p. 118.

27 *Home Office v Harman* (1982), 1 A11 ER 532.

28 *British Steel Corporation Ltd v Granada Television* (1980), 3 WLR 774.

29 Sir James Goldsmith, *The Communist Propaganda Apparatus and Other Threats to the Media* (1981), p. 10.

30 Royal Commission on the Press, Cmnd. 6810 (1977), Chapter 20 paragraph 2.

31 'Answers to Second Questionnaire by the Royal Commission on the Press' (Press Council 1975).

32 'Press Conduct in the Sutcliffe Case' (Press Council 1983), Chapter 6 paragraph 3.

33 *AG v Sunday Times and other newspapers* (1983).

34 'Press Conduct in the Sutcliffe Case', *op cit.*, Chapter 10 paragraph 34.

35 'Sunday Standard – Improper to Publish', *UK Press Gazette*, 14 March 1983, p 28.

36 *The Sunday Times v United Kingdom* (1979), European Human Rights Report, No. 2 p. 245.

6. *Press Monopolies*

1 Royal Commission on the Press, Cmnd. 7700 (49), paragraph 274.

2 *Ibid.*, paragraph 605.

3 *Ibid.*, paragraph 663.

4 'The Press and the People' (1960), pp. 23–4.

5 'The Press and the People' (1961), p. 13.

6 'The Press and the People' (1963), p. 17.

7 Royal Commission on the Press, Cmnd. 1811 (1962), paragraphs 323–4.

8 *Ibid.*, paragraph 326.

9 *Ibid.*, paragraph 341.

10   Fair Trading Act (1973), S59(3).
11   For an account of Press Council opposition, see H. Phillip Levy,
       The Press Council (Macmillan 1967), pp. 408–19.
12   *Associated Press v The United States* 326, US 1, p. 19.
13   'The Press and the People' (1968), p. 128.
14   The Monopolies Commission: '*The Times* Newspaper and the
       Sunday Times newspaper', (1966), House of Commons paper
       No. 273; see especially paragraphs 162–3 and 176.
15   H. Phillip Levy, *The Press Council* (Macmillan 1967).
16   'The Press and the People' (1973), p. 3.
17   The Westminster Press Ltd and Kentish Times Ltd, Gravesend and
       Dartford Reporter Ltd and F.J. Parsons Ltd, subsidiaries of
       Morgan–Grampian Ltd – House of Commons Paper No. 460,
       Session 1972–73.
18   'The Press and the People' (1973), p. 78.
19   'The Press and the People' (1974), p. 103.
20   Press Release (27 January 1981), No. 1315. The Secretary of State's
       decision is announced in *Hansard*, 27 January 1981, HC No. 34.
21   Fair Trading Act (1973), S58(3)(a).
22   Press Release (29 January 1981).
23   The *Observer* and George Outram & Co. Ltd, House of Commons
       Paper No. 378, Session 1981, Chapter 6 paragraphs 46–51.
24   Thomson Newspapers Ltd, *op. cit.*
25   The *Observer, op. cit.*, Chapter 8 paragraph 33.
26   Fair Trading Act (1973), S58(3).
27   Fair Trading Act (1973), S58(3)(a).
28   Fair Trading Act (1973), S58(3)(b).
29   Fair Trading Act (1975), S59(3).
30   Royal Commission on the Press, Cmnd. 6810 (1977), Chapter 14
       paragraph 28.
31   The *Observer, op. cit.*, Chapter 8 paragraphs 28–9.
32   Fair Trading Act (1973), S61(1)(b).
33   Fair Trading Act (1973), Schedule 3 paragraph 22.

7. Reform of the Press Council

1   *The Spectator,* 25 September 1982, p. 6.
2   Royal Commission on the Press, Cmnd. 6810 (1977), Chapter 17
       paragraphs 32–41.
3   *Mawe v Pigott* (1869), IR 4.
4   *Hansard,* 18 February 1983, Col. 602.
5   *Grapelli v Derek Block* (1981), 2 All ER 272.
6   *Boston v Bagshaw & Sons* (1966), 1 WLR 1126.

7   *The Times,* letter to the Editor, 22 June 1976. See Geoffrey
     Robertson, 'Law for the Press' in Curran (ed.), *The British Press
     – a Manifesto* (Macmillan 1978).

8   Parliamentary Commissioner Act, 1967.

9   R. Gregory & P. G. Hutcheson, *The Parliamentary Ombudsman*
     (1975).

10   Newspaper Libel and Registration Act, (1881), S2; and see Gatley,
     Libel and Slander (Sweet and Maxwell 1981), p. 277.

11   Law of Libel Amendment Act (1888), S4.

12   Defamation Act (1952), S7 and Schedule thereto.

13   Report of the Committee on Defamation, Cmnd. 5909 (1975),
     paragraphs 227 *et seq.*

14   'Review of the UK Self-Regulatory System of Advertising Control'
     (Office of Fair Trading 1978).

15   Advertising Standards Authority, Annual Report 1981, p. 5 and
     pp. 20–3.

16   'Self-discipline not State Discipline', *The Times* Editorial,
     18 February 1983.

17   Royal Commission on the Press, Cmnd. 1811 (1962), paragraph
     325.

18   'Press Conduct in the Sutcliffe Case' (Press Council 1983), Chapter
     18 paragraph 5.

19   Royal Commission on the Press, Cmnd. 7700 (1949), paragraph
     634.

20   Brian Lapping (ed.), *The Bounds of Freedom,* (Constable, 1980).

21   Broadcasting Act (1981), Part III, S53–60; Report of the Broad-
     casting Complaints Commission (HMSO 1982); Geoffrey
     Robertson, 'The Broadcasting Complaints Commission', *The
     Listener,* 11 September, 13 November 1980.

22   *Thames Television v Broadcasting Complaints Commission* (1982),
     decision of Stephen Brown J.

23   Lennart Groll (the first Swedish Press Ombudsman): 'Freedom and
     Self-discipline of the Swedish Press' (Swedish Institute 1980);
     'Legal Constraints on the Press: Swedish and British
     Viewpoints', Lennart Groll and Geoffrey Robertson, in
     Freedom and the Press (Department of Visual Communication,
     Goldsmiths College, 1979).

24   Royal Commission on the Press, Cmnd. 6810 (1977), Chapter 20
     paragraphs 30–35.

25   'The Press and the People' (1979), p. 1.

26   The *Guardian,* Editorial, 4 February 1983.

27   *Hansard,* 18 February 1983, HC No. 62, Col. 630.

28   *Ibid.,* Col. 628.

29 *Ibid.*, Col. 630.
30 'The Press and the People' (1979), paragraph 39.
31 Contempt of Court Act (1981), S10.

Index